IGCSE

English as a Second Language Workbook 2

Third edition

Peter Lucantoni

CAMBRIDGE
UNIVERSITY PRESS

CAMBRIDGE UNIVERSITY PRESS
Cambridge, New York, Melbourne, Madrid, Cape Town, Singapore,
São Paulo, Delhi

Cambridge University Press
The Edinburgh Building, Cambridge CB2 8RU, UK

www.cambridge.org
Information on this title: www.cambridge.org/9780521736039

First published 2005
Third edition 2008

Printed in the United Kingdom at the University Press, Cambridge

A catalogue record for this publication is available from the British Library

ISBN 978-0-521-73603-9 paperback

ACKNOWLEDGEMENTS

Cover image: © ImageState/Alamy

I would like to thank the students and teachers, from all over the world,
who have used this book, and who have provided me with so much
positive feedback. Thanks also to those of you who have pointed out
errors in the second edition, and to those who have made suggestions
for improvements – I hope I have been able to include your ideas in this
third edition.

As always, final thanks and all my love go to Lydia, Sara and Emily, who
continue to support my efforts – I couldn't do it without you.

Contents

Menu

Introduction

The new edition of this Workbook is for students who are taking the International General Certificate of Secondary Education (IGCSE) English as a Second Language (E2L) examination, and has been written to supplement the new edition of Coursebook 2.

It is assumed that most of you who use this book will be studying English in order to improve your educational or employment prospects, and it therefore includes topics and themes relevant to this goal. You will find passages and activities based on a wide variety of stimulating topics and about people from all over the world, which I hope you will enjoy reading and discussing.

The Workbook follows the same procedure as the Coursebook, with each themed unit focusing on a specific aspect of the IGCSE E2L examination. Furthermore, the Workbook units reinforce areas of language, as well as providing more opportunities for you to research and complete projects. In addition, each unit offers practice in writing skills.

There are four units (5, 10, 15 and 20) providing examination practice, helping you to build your confidence and develop the additional skills and techniques necessary for success in the examination.

I hope you enjoy using this book!

Peter Lucantoni

Unit 1:
Focus on reading skills

Exam Exercise 1

Vocabulary

1   Think back to Unit 1 of your Coursebook. How many different leisure activities can you remember? Make a list and then look in your Coursebook to check.

2   In Unit 1, you looked at six different endings for adjectives. What are they? Make a list and give two examples for each ending.

Reading 1

3   In Unit 1 of the Coursebook, you practised finding key words in questions. Look at the questions below and think about what the key words (or word) are in each question. You do not need to write anything yet. If you are working with a classmate, discuss the reasons for your choices.

   a   How many methods of transport are available to reach the Isles of Scilly?
   b   What is *Scillonian III*?
   c   Name **four** 'treasures' of the islands.
   d   Which other part of the world are the islands compared with?
   e   How many people live on the Isles of Scilly?
   f   What do you need to do before travelling between any of the islands?
   g   On which island is the Old Wesleyan Chapel?
   h   Where can you find the second-oldest lighthouse in Britain?

   Write down the **type** of answer which each of the above questions requires. For example, the answer to Question a is going to be a number because the question asks '**How many** methods of transport ... ?'

4   Skim-read the article about the Isles of Scilly and find the answers to the questions in Exercise 3. Do not write anything yet.

Exam tip

Remember that, in this part of the examination, you need to keep your answers short. In some cases, you may need to write only one word, or a number. Some questions may require you to give more than a single piece of information, as in Question c of Exercise 3. When this is the case, try to write each piece of information on a separate line. The important thing is to work quickly and not to waste time repeating the question in your answer.

Part 1

Remember that you will not be required to answer questions based on parts of the text which contain unusual vocabulary. The words *cairns* in line 6 and *launches* in line 10 are unusual, but you do not need to know what they mean in order to answer any of the questions in Exercise 3. (Note: a *cairn* is a pile of stones, often used in the past as a memorial or to show where someone was buried; a *launch* is a type of boat, usually for transporting groups of people.)

Discover the Isles of Scilly by air or sea

The Isles of Scilly Steamship Group provides you with two great choices to enjoy a day trip to the islands.

Whether you choose to cruise on *Scillonian III* or to fly on Skybus (the islands' own airline), and whatever time of year you visit, you will be sure to enjoy the natural beauty of the islands.

Exotic plants and wild flowers, ancient cairns and crumbling castles, sparkling white sands and an azure sea – all the treasures of the islands await you. Only 28 miles from England's Land's End, but with a real hint of the Tropics.

The Isles are populated by a community of 2,000 islanders and there are five inhabited islands to explore to make your day trip one to remember. Inter-island launches are available from St Mary's quay. Check times and tides for availability.

St Mary's, where the airport is situated, is the largest of the islands. Hugh Town, its capital, is the commercial centre and offers a great choice of shops, restaurants and cafés. You will find the Tourist Information Centre at the Old Wesleyan Chapel in Hugh Town. Don't miss the exhibits at the museum or a walk round the Garrison and the Elizabethan fort, now known as the Star Castle Hotel. There are many walks, nature trails and safe white sand beaches.

The other inhabited islands are St Martin's, Bryher, Tresco and St Agnes. On the latter is a 17th-century lighthouse, the second oldest in Britain, as well as an inn and a café for refreshments. The beaches at Porth Conger and the Cove are great for swimming.

5   Which of the following would be the **best** response to Question **a** of Exercise 3? Why?

    a   *There are two methods of transport available to reach the Isles of Scilly.*
    b   *Two.*
    c   *There are two.*
    d   *To reach the Isles of Scilly there are two methods of transport.*

6   Write answers to the other questions in Exercise 3.

 ## Research

7   The text you have just read talks about a group of islands off the coast of Great Britain. Use an atlas to find these islands. Then look around the rest of the coast and see how many other islands you can find.

8   Think about a country with an island or islands, with which you are familiar. Then find out as much information as you can about the islands. Use the Scilly Isles text as a guide.

 ## Writing 1

9   Use the information you researched in Exercise 8 to write a description of the island or islands. Try to include information about climate, vegetation, population, important towns, geographical position, and so on. Write between 150 and 200 words.

Reading 2

10 You are going to read some information taken from a leaflet about Venizelos Airport, the international airport in Athens. The leaflet contains information for people with special needs who may face some difficulties in the airport environment. What type of information do you think the leaflet might contain? Make a list.

Example: *special car-parking facilities*

11 Here is a list of the headings contained in the leaflet. There are also two extra headings which are **not** in the leaflet. Compare the headings with your ideas from Exercise 10. Did you think of the same things? Which two headings do you think are **not** in the leaflet?

First Aid	Shopping
Free telephones and information desks	Special check-in counters and waiting areas
Parking	Special drop-off/pick-up spaces
Passport control	Toilets

12 Read the leaflet on page **4** and choose the best heading from Exercise **11** for each of the gaps.

13 The two headings which are not in the leaflet are 'Passport control' and 'Shopping'. If they were in the leaflet, what information do you think these sections might contain? Write a few sentences for each one.

 # Writing 2

14 Here are some headings for a speech you are going to give about the facilities at Venizelos Airport for people with special needs. In your notebook, write short notes under each heading, using the information from the text.

Outside the airport building	**Inside the airport building**
• dedicated drop-off spaces	•
• pavements have …	•
•	• signs and notices in Braille
•	• four First Aid rooms
•	•
	•

VENIZELOS AIRPORT, ATHENS – assistance for people with special needs

(a) _____

Easy access to the main airport building is provided through dedicated spaces in front of all the central entrances of both the Arrivals and Departures levels. Please note that all pavements have wheelchair ramps.

(b) _____

Adequate parking space in convenient locations: 36 in front of the main airport building and 101 in the airport car parks. Additionally, the long-term-parking shuttle buses are equipped with ramps, and further assistance is available on request.

(c) _____

Depending on airline arrangements, you are welcome to check in at dedicated check-in counters next to Entrance 2 at the Departures level.

(d) _____

Toilets for disabled people are available in all airport areas. Signs and notices are provided in Braille.

(e) _____

Four First Aid rooms are available at the airport, equipped to deal with minor incidents. Emergency incidents can be handled immediately at the medical station of the Hellenic Centre of First Aid. For more information, please go to one of the Information desks, ask any of the airport employees, or use the special free telephones.

(f) _____

In the main airport building (close to the Information desks) there are 16 telephones with free direct connection to the airport's call centre. Disabled people have easy access to these phones; furthermore, text phones for people with hearing problems are provided.

Language

15 What does *whether ... or* mean in the sentence below, which is taken from the text on page **2**?

> **Whether** *you choose to cruise on* Scillonian III **or** *to fly on Skybus ... you will be sure to enjoy ... .*

Look at this example:

> **Whether** *we go on holiday this week* **or** *next week, it'll cost the same.*

Write **five** sentences of your own to show that you understand how to use *whether ... or.*

16 All the words in the table below are taken from the two texts in this unit.

Copy the table and complete as many gaps as possible. Remember that you may not be able to complete all the gaps.

Adjective	Adjective opposite	Noun	Verb	Adverb
	ugly	beauty		
exotic				
inhabited				
available				
commercial				
		access		
				additionally
		assistance		
medical				
special				

17 Look at this sentence from the text on page **3** of your Coursebook:

This is the one that sold a million in a month.

Introductory phrase	Noun	Relative pronoun	Verb phrase
This is the	*one*	*that*	*sold a million in a month.*
This/That is the ... These/Those are the ...	person/people woman/women film/films car/cars team/teams year/years reason/reasons (etc.)	who when which why that where	

Use the words in the table above to write **five** sentences. There are many different possibilities. You will need to complete the final verb phrase yourself.

Example: *Those are the / reasons / why / he left the country.*

18 Look at this phrase from the text on page **9** of your Coursebook:

Located only minutes from the Falls, the hotel has splendid views ... .

This information could also be written as:

The hotel is located only minutes from the Falls and has splendid views ... .

Rewrite the following information in the same style as the phrase from your Coursebook, beginning each phrase with either an *-ed* or an *-ing* participle.

a This hotel is regarded as one of the best on the African continent and has been voted the best in Zimbabwe.

Regarded as ......

b Your evening starts with a meal cooked by our head chef and continues with a programme of African music and dance.

Starting with ......

c The hotel offers a full range of 5★ facilities, including its own cinema, as well as a pool complex with diving boards.

Offering ......

19 Write **five** sentences of your own. Each sentence should begin with either an *-ed* or an *-ing* participle.

VOCABULARY BOX

Braille

A Frenchman, Louis Braille, who was blind from the age of three, devised the Braille system in about 1830. He lived from 1809 to 1852, and during his life was a musician and a teacher.

castle

This comes from the Latin word *castellum*, which meant 'fortified village'. The word has changed over the years and once had the form -*chester* in place names (e.g. Manchester, Winchester). The Spanish kingdom of Castile takes its name from the original Latin word *castellum*.

passport

A very literal word originating from the French *passer*, meaning 'to pass', and the word *port* from the Latin *portus*, which refers to a point of crossing for transport and people.

shuttle

This word originally referred to a dart, harpoon or arrow, from an old German word *skutilaz*, meaning 'shoot' or 'move across'. Today, we see the word used in transport and also in the word *shuttlecock* from the game of badminton.

Unit 2:
Focus on reading skills

Exam Exercise 2

 ## Vocabulary

1   In Unit **2** of the Coursebook, you read a text about young people in France. Look at these definitions of five of the words you read, and try to remember what the original words in the text were. The first letter of each word has been given, as well as the number of letters.

    a older or superior person   e _ _ _ _
    b university teacher   a _ _ _ _ _ _ _
    c show something off   f _ _ _ _ _
    d conveniently close   h _ _ _ _
    e extremely, tremendously   o _ _ _ _ _ _ _ _ _ _ _ _

2   Use the words from Exercise **1** to complete these five sentences from the text. You may need to change the form of some of the words. Then try to order the sentences as they were in the text.

    a *Many ...... , teachers and parents complain because they feel that intellectual levels are falling rapidly!*
    b *For 90% of young people aged 14 to 18, radio is also ...... popular: they listen to it every day without exception.*
    c *They have their own culture, which they ...... without any hang-ups about it!*
    d *Young people do, of course, watch a lot of television, but less than their ....*
    e *... while watching American soaps such as* Friends *or reality shows like* Star Academy *on television, music player glued to their ears, and the games console ....*

 ## Reading 1

3   Look at the map of Europe on page **8**, which shows how a deadly disease (plague) spread across the continent during the 14th century. What do the different shades on the map tell you?

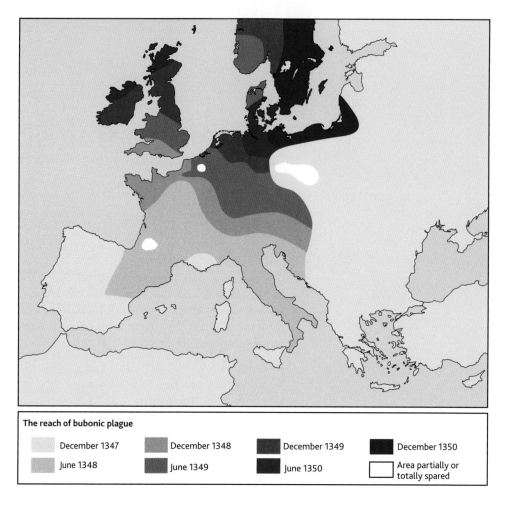

The reach of bubonic plague

	December 1347		December 1348		December 1349		December 1350
	June 1348		June 1349		June 1350		Area partially or totally spared

4 Look at the table. Match the words and phrases in column **A**, which are taken from the text 'Scientists decipher DNA code of plague', with a suitable definition in column **B**. There are two extra definitions which you do not need to use. Use your dictionary to help you.

A	B
a *bug* (paragraph 6)	causes
b *deciphered* (1)	deadly
c *devastated* (6)	greatly damaged
d *lethal* (6)	different types
e *microbe* (1)	expectations
f *poses* (2)	germ
g *resistant to* (2)	infection
h *rodents* (3)	made sense of
i *strains* (2)	rats
j *wiped out* (4)	killed
	security
	unaffected by

5 Now skim the text below. Find the words from Column **A** in Exercise **4**. Do the definitions you chose from Column **B** make sense?

6 Read the following questions and find the key word/s in each one. You do **not** need to write anything yet.

    a What is the name of the bacterium whose code has been deciphered?

    b Apart from being resistant to drugs, what other threat does the bacterium pose to humans?

    c When did the plague first affect Europe?

    d Where does modern plague survive today and how is it transferred to humans?

    e List **four** other diseases whose genetic codes have been deciphered by scientists.

    f What effect did the Black Death have on Europe in the 14th century?

    g In which direction did the plague travel across Europe in the 14th century?

    h How was the vet infected with pneumonic plague?

    i What form did the plague probably take until 1,500 years ago?

    j Name the **two** varieties of plague known to scientists.

    k Why was bubonic plague originally called 'Pasteuralla pestis'?

    l When and where were 855 people killed by pneumonic plague?

7 Skim the text again and try to find the key words you identified in the questions in Exercise **6**.

8 Write your answers to the questions in Exercise **6**. Remember to keep your answers as brief as possible, but include all the necessary information.

Part 1

Scientists decipher DNA code of plague

By Tim Radford, Science Editor

(1) Scientists have deciphered the entire genetic code of one of the great diseases of mankind – the plague. The 465 million 'letters' of the DNA of a bacterium (or microbe) called 'Yersinia pestis' could begin to answer questions about a disease that changed history at least three times – and could do so again.

(2) The recent identification of strains of plague resistant to drugs, and the possibility of using the microbe 'Yersinia pestis' as a chemical weapon in a war, mean that plague still poses a threat to humans.

(3) Plague affected Europe in the 6th and 8th centuries, as well as repeatedly between the 14th and 18th centuries (when it was known as the 'Black Death'), and it continues to cause problems in the 21st century. It survives in groups of rodents and is carried to humans by the bite of an infected insect. Plague is not the first killer disease to be identified and deciphered – scientists already have the genetic codes for cholera, malaria, leprosy, meningitis and many others. But plague has been the most dramatic killer of all.

(4) The Black Death is believed to have wiped out one third of Europe's population as it spread westwards from the Far East across the continent in the 14th century. The World Health Organization receives reports of up to 3,000 infections each year. The deadly bacterium lives in populations of rats in Asia and the western United States of America, and from time to time it spreads to city rats in other parts of the world.

(5) The strain used to decipher the plague code came from a vet who died in 1992 after a cat with pneumonic plague sneezed on him. He was trying to rescue the cat from underneath a house at the time. Many people do not realise that plague is still with us, although it is not nearly as common as it used to be.

(6) The microbe probably began in the form of a stomach infection and developed into something much more lethal around 1,500 years ago. It has adopted a different lifestyle in a remarkably short space of time, changing basically from a stomach bug to a killer disease that has devastated the world.

(*continues on page 10 …*)

(... continued)

(7) The DNA code of plague will help researchers looking for new drugs and medicines. One medicine is already being tested. Plague has also been proposed as a possible chemical weapon.

(8) The facts of death

Plague lives in two forms: the lethal pneumonic variety, spread by coughing and sneezing; the other is the bubonic variety, which exists mostly in America, Africa and Asia. This latter variety was identified in 1894 by a scientist called Alexandre Yersin, who originally named it 'Pasteuralla pestis' after his teacher, Louis Pasteur. The last big outbreak of pneumonic plague, in India in 1992, killed 855 people. The last outbreak in London was the Great Plague of 1665.

Adapted from an article by Tim Radford in *The Guardian*, 4 October 2001.

 ## Research

9 Look again at the DNA text and find and note down all the technical words and phrases; for example, *genetic code* (paragraph 1). Use a bilingual dictionary to check what these words and phrases are in your own language.

10 Use the information in the text to draw a time graph or chart. Your teacher will help you to get started.

 ## Writing 1

11 In Exercise 10, you put information from the DNA text into graphical form. Now use this information as a basis to write about the events.

 ## Reading 2

12 You are going to read an article about an archaeological discovery in Greece. The text contains some vocabulary which you may not know. Here are eleven words and phrases which have been removed from the text. Use your dictionary to check the meaning of each one. Do not look at the text yet. Write down the meanings of each word.

a *exploits*	e *myths*	i *stumbled across*
b *mundane*	f *painstaking*	j *determination*
c *excavating*	g *settlement*	k *perplexed*
d *composite*	h *quest*	

13 Here are the meanings (not in the right order) which fit the words and phrases in Exercise 12. Check your answers.

strength	digging out	legends
careful	puzzled	routine
community	discovered	activities
complex	expedition	

Now use these 'meanings' to complete the grid on page 11. The letters in the shaded area will reveal an important word from the text.

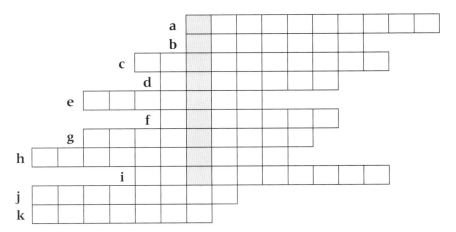

14 Copy the grid. Skim the text. Use the words from Exercise **12** to complete each gap. Make sure you use the context (the phrases before and after each gap) to help you.

15 Read the following questions and find the key word/s in each one.

    a What have archaeologists found in central Greece?
    b What is the shape of a 'tholos'?
    c When was the community first discovered?
    d How did Vasso Adrimi feel when she examined the site?
    e Who encouraged Vasso in her search?
    f What has helped Ms Adrimi to put together the evidence she needs?
    g What does she think the legend of Jason may be based on?
    h Name **three** items made using the moulds which Ms Adrimi found.

16 Now write the answers to the questions in Exercise **15**.

Golden legend unearthed in Greece

High in the foothills of central Greece, evidence is emerging that may explain one of the world's longest-lasting **(a)** .... Archaeologists are **(b)** ...... the remains of what they believe is ancient Iolcus, the city which Jason and the Argonauts departed from to find the Golden Fleece.

Located on a former vegetable field in the Thessalian village of Dimini, the excavation lies below an important neolithic **(c)** ...... from more than 7,000 years ago, long before the age of the Greek heroes. This particular excavation site also has a 'tholos': a beehive-shaped tomb (a place for burying people), which is associated with Mycenaean culture 3,200 to 3,600 years ago.

Vasso Adrimi discovered the large Mycenaean settlement in central Greece nearly 25 years ago. But linking reality to legend was no easy business. 'I spent two months examining the site and was most **(d)** ...... ,' she says. 'It came as a shock, a very big shock, when my professor linked the site to the two Mycenean royal 'tholos' tombs we also have here. He said: "Keep going, I have no doubt that this is the ancient Mycenean city of Iolcus. You have **(e)** ...... the find of your life,"' says Ms Adrimi, who kept going with great **(f)** ....

Now, assisted by modern technology, she has pieced together enough evidence to suggest that the Jason legend may have been based on the **(g)** ...... of a seafaring people who sailed on the Black Sea.

'We may never know who Jason was, or if he ever existed, but I think it is safe to say the myth of the Argonauts is the product of historical memory, dressed up with lots of dramatic fiction,' she says.

Ms Adrimi belongs to a small group in Greece who believe in 'breaking the barrier of time' by studying even the most **(h)** ...... aspects of ancient life. Hers is a **(i)** ...... method of enquiry, which is not interested in the glory that goes in hand with a more sensational type of archaeological find.

The claim of identifying Iolcus is based on a **(j)** ...... picture of life around a palace, but it was the discovery of moulds for making jewellery, weapons and tools that set her thinking. 'The raw materials, like gold, obviously needed to be obtained from somewhere – maybe the myth of the Argonauts was inspired by the memory of the **(k)** ...... to bring them back.'

Adapted from an article by Helena Smith in *The Guardian Weekly,* 11–17 October 2001.

Writing 2

17 Imagine that you have visited the village of Dimini and have seen the remains of Iolcus. Write a letter to an English-speaking friend telling him or her what you saw there. Write between 150 and 200 words (Extended) or between 100 and 150 (Core).

 ## Language

18 Look at the table. Read the phrases in column **A**. They are linked to the two texts you have already read in this unit, although some of them are used in a different sense. Which words or phrases from column **B** match the phrases in column **A**? Some words and phrases in column **B** cannot be used. The phrases in column **A** will match with either one or two words or phrases.

A		B
a	made into an understandable language (2 words or phrases)	deadly
b	caused great destruction (2)	deciphered
c	causing death (2)	greatly damaged
d	the word originates from Greek and means 'small life' (1)	devastated
e	sits for a photograph (1)	different types
f	hostile to (1)	germ
g	animals which often carry disease (2)	lethal
h	stretches something tightly (1)	made sense of
i	taken off (1)	microbe
		poses
		rats
		killed
		resistant to
		rodents
		strains
		unaffected by
		wiped out

19 Choose **five** words or phrases from Exercise **18** and use them in sentences of your own.

Example: *She made no sense of his writing because it was so awful.*

20 What does *latter* mean in the sentence below, which is taken from paragraph **8** of the DNA text on pages **9–10**?

> *This latter variety was identified ... .*

Look at these examples:

- *Plague lives in two forms: pneumonic and bubonic. The former is spread by coughing; the latter is found in Asia.*
- *There are two main sources of water: underground rivers and man-made dams. The former can be found all over the island while the latter have been built in areas of high rainfall.*

Write **five** sentences of your own to show that you understand how to use *former* and *latter*.

21 The two texts in this unit refer to events which happened long ago. Often these types of text use the passive form of the verb (*to be* + past participle).

Examples: *The Black Death is believed to have wiped out a third of the population.*

The claim of identifying Iolcus is based on a ... .

Unjumble the words and phrases in the table below to make meaningful sentences. Put each verb into its correct passive form. Don't worry if you are not sure about the correct dates!

a	The Solar System (form)	by dinosaurs	in 1961
b	The planet Earth (dominate)	by Marconi	in the 16th century
c	Copper and gold (use)	to Europe by rats	in the 18th century
d	Bubonic plague (bring)	by only five million people worldwide	in 1894
e	English (speak)	to Europe from Latin America	in 2004
f	Rubber (bring)	in Athens, Greece,	around 1346
g	The radio (invent)	into space	during the Bronze Age
h	The first man, Yuri Gagarin, (launch)	by man	about 4,600 million years ago
i	The Olympic Games (hold)	by gases	about 235 million years ago

22 In this unit you have seen these abbreviations: IGCSE, DNA. What do they stand for?

> IGCSE   International General Certificate of Secondary Education
> DNA   deoxyribonucleic acid

Now find out what these abbreviations stand for, and write them in full. Use your dictionary to help you.

a	WHO	**c**	DVD	**e**	UNICEF	**g**	SMS
b	BBC	**d**	VCR	**f**	NATO	**h**	UFO

VOCABULARY BOX

disease
This is an interesting word made up from two Old French words: *des-* + *-aise*, **without** + **ease**. The original meaning was 'discomfort' or 'uncomfortable'. It was first used to mean 'sickness' in 1393.

legend
From a Latin word *legenda*, meaning 'story' or 'things to be read'.

plague
This word originates from the Latin *plaga*, meaning 'disease', and was used in English as long ago as 1382.

Unit 3:
Focus on writing skills

Exam Exercises 6 and 7

 ## Vocabulary

1   Here are some types of food from Unit 3 in your Coursebook. Unjumble the letters and then write the types of food in either the 'Fast food' or 'Traditional food' column.

rugerb   shoulag   chindsaw   crie   kamasous   lefalaf   asomas

Fast food	Traditional food

2   Use the words below to complete the gaps in the following paragraph. Then check your answers using the 'Pasta gives way to present' text on page 21 of the Coursebook.

turnover   gourmets   decades   ambience   palate   launched   outlets

(a) ...... of resistance by family-owned bars, pizzerias and restaurants look like ending in defeat with the announcement that the two chains are doubling their **(b)** ...... in Italy.

McDonald's says that the **(c)** ...... at its existing 243 restaurants jumped by almost 20% last year ... Two months ago, the chain **(d)** ...... its first pizza in Italy, called Pizza Mia.

'It is the globalisation of the **(e)** ...... ,' *La Repubblica* mourned ... Breakdowns of ingredients and a calorie count (610) were accompanied by warnings from leading **(f)** ....

'The **(g)** ...... was mechanical, the chips like cardboard and the bread poor.'

 ## Reading 1

3   You are going to read an article on page 17 about veganism. Before you read, look at the following words and phrases from the text. Match each one with a suitable definition in the opposite column. Use your dictionary to help you.

Words and phrases	Definition
absorption (paragraph j)	developed or coming from something else
adequate (e)	enough, sufficient
chronic (f)	meat from birds such as chicken and ducks
conform to (f)	milk, cheese, butter, etc.
dairy foods (a)	not containing
derived from (a)	not treating animals and people in a cruel way
free of (f)	obey a rule
humane (c)	obeying all the rules
poultry (a)	only a little
sparingly (f)	process where something takes in something else
strict (e)	continuing for a long time

4   These sentences and phrases are taken from or are based on the article. Use the words from Exercise **3** to complete the gaps.

   a *Vegetarians do not eat meat, fish or ....*
   b *Vegans do not use other animal products, such as honey, eggs and ....*
   c *Cosmetics and soaps are ...... animal products.*
   d *Many vegans choose this lifestyle to promote a more ...... and caring world.*
   e *It is easy for a vegan diet to meet the recommendations for protein as long as calorie intake is ....*
   f *...... protein planning or combining is not necessary.*
   g *Vegan diets are ...... cholesterol and are generally low in fat.*
   h *Thus, eating a vegan diet makes it easy to ...... recommendations given to reduce the risk of major ...... diseases such as cancer.*
   i *High-fat foods, which should be used ...... , include oils and nuts.*
   j *Iron ...... is increased markedly by eating foods containing vitamin C.*

5   Skim the article. Find and underline the words and phrases from Exercise **3**.

6   There are eleven short paragraphs in the article. Each paragraph has a heading. Read the headings below and decide which one goes with each paragraph.

Calcium	Iron	What is a vegan?
Caring	Protein	Why veganism?
Fat	Vegan nutrition	Zinc
For more information	Vitamin D	

   Additional questions

   Now write the answers to the following questions, based on the information provided in the article.

   a Which three food types contain similar quantities of iron?
   b Which food type contains approximately two times as much iron mg/cup as green beans?

Why not become a vegan?

(a) _____

Vegetarians do not eat meat, fish or poultry. Vegans, in addition to being vegetarian, do not use other animal products, such as honey, eggs and dairy foods, nor animal by-products; for example, leather, fur, silk, wool, cosmetics and soaps derived from animal products.

(b) _____

People choose to be vegan for health, environmental and/or ethical reasons. For example, some vegans feel that, by consuming eggs and dairy products, the meat industry is promoted. That is, once dairy cows or egg-laying chickens are too old to be productive, they are often sold as meat; and since male calves do not produce milk, they are usually raised for veal or other meat products. Some people avoid these items because of the conditions associated with their production.

(c) _____

Many vegans choose this lifestyle to promote a more humane and caring world. They know that they are not perfect, but believe that they have a responsibility to try to do their best, while not being judgemental of others.

(d) _____

The key to a nutritionally sound vegan diet is variety. A healthy and varied vegan diet includes fruits, vegetables, plenty of leafy greens, wholegrain products, nuts, seeds and legumes.

(e) _____

It is very easy for a vegan diet to meet the recommendations for protein as long as calorie intake is adequate. Strict protein planning or combining is not necessary. The key is to eat a varied diet. Almost all foods, except for sugar and fats, are good sources of protein. Vegan sources include: potatoes, wholewheat bread, rice, broccoli, spinach, almonds, peas, chickpeas, peanut butter, tofu, soy milk, lentils, kale. For example, if part of a day's menu included the following foods, you would meet the Recommended Dietary Allowance (RDA) for protein for an adult male: 1 cup oatmeal, 1 cup soy milk, 2 slices wholewheat bread, 1 bagel, 2 tablespoons peanut butter, 1 cup vegetarian baked beans, 5 ounces tofu, 2 tablespoons almonds, 1 cup broccoli and 1 cup brown rice.

(f) _____

Vegan diets are free of cholesterol and are generally low in fat. Thus, eating a vegan diet makes it easy to conform to recommendations given to reduce the risk of major chronic diseases such as heart disease and cancer. High-fat foods, which should be used sparingly, include oils, margarine, nuts, nut butters, seed butters, avocados and coconuts.

(g) _____

Vitamin D is not found in the vegan diet but can be made by humans with at least ten to fifteen minutes of summer sun on the hands and face two to three times a week. This is recommended for adults so that vitamin D production can occur.

(h) _____

Calcium, needed for strong bones, is found in dark-green vegetables, tofu processed with calcium sulphate, and many other foods commonly eaten by vegans. Calcium requirements for those on lower-protein, plant-based diets may be somewhat lower than requirements for those eating a higher-protein, flesh-based diet. However, it is important for vegans to eat foods high in calcium and/or use a vegan calcium supplement every day.

(i) _____

Vegan diets can provide zinc at levels close to or even higher than the RDA. Zinc is found in grains, legumes and nuts.

(j) _____

Dried beans and dark-green vegetables are especially good sources of iron (see chart), better on a per-calorie basis than meat. Iron absorption is increased markedly by eating foods containing vitamin C along with foods containing iron.

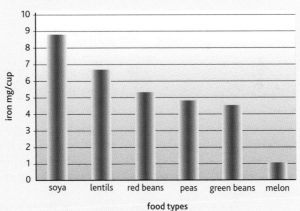

(k) _____

Order *Simply Vegan* for a complete discussion of vegan nutrition plus 160 quick and easy recipes. This excellent resource contains over 160 vegan recipes that can be prepared quickly. An extensive vegan nutrition section by Reed Mangels, PhD, RD, covers topics such as protein, fat, calcium, iron, vitamin B12, pregnancy and the vegan diet, feeding vegan kids, weight gain and weight loss, and provides a nutrition glossary. Also featured are sample menus and meal plans. *Simply Vegan* is more than a cookbook. An additional section on mail-order shopping tells you where to find vegan clothes, non-leather shoes, cosmetics, household products and books.

Adapted from www.vrg.org, 18 January 2004.

Research

7   There are many types of food mentioned in the text on page 17 with which you may be unfamiliar; for example, veal in paragraph **b** or chickpeas in paragraph **e**. Use a bilingual dictionary to find out what these are in your own language.

8   In paragraph **e**, there are some units of measurement with which you may be unfamiliar. Find out what the following units are in the metric system.

   a   1 cup
   b   2 tablespoons
   c   5 ounces

 ## Writing 1

9   In Exercises **18** and **19** of Unit **3** of the Coursebook, you reviewed phrases used to express opinion. Imagine that your friend is thinking of becoming a vegan. Write an informal letter to her/him expressing your opinion about veganism. Write between 150 and 200 words and include in your letter information about:

   • the kind of people who become vegans
   • the products that vegans eat and use
   • why you think veganism would / would not suit your friend.

 ## Reading 2

10   You are going to read a passage about obesity on page **19**. First, look at these questions and make some brief notes. Use your dictionary to help you.

   a   What does 'obesity' mean?
   b   What do you think causes obesity?
   c   In which countries do most people suffer from obesity? Why?
   d   Do you think the levels of obesity are changing? Why?

11   Which of these words do you think will appear in the text? Write down your choices and try to give reasons for your answers. Use your dictionary to help you.

   businessmen   teenagers   fashion   friends
   smoking   gym   advertising   Asia   tiger
   bomb   chocolate   carbohydrate   prosperity

12   Skim the text and check your word choices in Exercise **11**.

13   Match the headings below to the paragraphs in the text on page **19**.

   Class and trends   Health dangers of obesity
   Statistics on the sales of fattening foods   Not just what you eat
   Shoppers' habits   Sales of healthier products

Obesity – fat of the land

The government worries that it should do something to change the way people eat. But diets are already changing.

Given mankind's need to worry, it is not surprising that the diseases of prosperity – stress, depression and, increasingly, obesity – get a lot of attention.

(a) _____
Obesity is a serious problem as it increases the risk of diabetes, heart disease and cancer. It is not clear what governments can do about it, and evidence suggests that the idea of imposing taxes on foods is not necessarily the answer. In Sweden, where advertising to young people is already banned, children are as overweight as they are in any comparable country.

(b) _____
Furthermore, it is not obvious that the problem will worsen. Shoppers' behaviour suggests the opposite. It is not just the flight from carbohydrates; there is a broader shift going on.

(c) _____
Companies are edging away from fattening foods. Five years ago, chocolate made up 80% of sales in a world-leading company; now, that is down to half. Five years ago, 85% of drinks sales were sweet, fizzy stuff. That's down to 56%. The rest is mostly juice. Diet drinks – which make up a third of the sales of fizzy drinks – are growing at 5% a year, while sales of the fattening stuff are static.

(d) _____
Supermarkets say that people are buying healthier foods. Lower-calorie ranges grew by 12% in 2003: twice the growth in overall sales. Sales of fruit and vegetables are growing faster than overall sales, too. Cafés and restaurants also report an increase in healthy eating. A sandwich store says that sales of salads grew by 63% last year.

(e) _____
But it isn't just eating too much fatty stuff that makes people fat. It's laziness, too. That may be changing. According to a market-research company, there were 3.8 million members of private gyms last year, up from 2.2 million in 1998. The average man got thinner in 2002.

(f) _____
Obesity is also seen as a class issue and, where the rich lead, the poor tend to follow – partly because the poor get richer over time, and partly because health messages tend to reach the better educated first and the worse educated later. That's what has been happening with smoking, a habit the rich gave up years ago and the poor are now stubbing out too. With younger consumers, peer pressure tends to have more impact than any amount of government intervention.

Adapted from *The Economist*, 6–12 March 2004.

Writing 2

14 Here are some notes based on each heading from Exercise **13**. Write a passage of about 150–200 words using the notes to guide you. Make sure you use the notes in the same order as the information appears in the text.

- Class and trends
  the poor follow the rich / smoking / peer pressure and government intervention

- Health dangers of obesity
  diseases / food taxes / Sweden

- Statistics on the sales of fattening foods
  chocolate sales / drinks

- Not just what you eat
  lifestyles / fitness clubs

- Shoppers' habits
  carbohydrates

- Sales of healthier products
  low-calorie foods / fruit and vegetables / cafés and restaurants

Language

15 There are various phrases which you can use to write about advantages and disadvantages. Copy the table below and add more phrases to the lists.

Advantages	Disadvantages
On the plus side ...	Another drawback is ...

16 The following two extracts are taken from the 'Shellfish in Oman' text on page **25** of your Coursebook. Look at how the **adverbs** *once* and *today* are used:

> *Once, abalone shellfish were brought to the surface ...*

> *Today, the shellfish are caught for ...*

Here, *once* means 'at some stage in the past', and *today* means 'at the present time'.

Write **eight** sentences which show you can correctly use these two adverbs.

17 Look at this sentence from the article about veganism on page **17**.

> *Vegans, in addition to being vegetarian, do not use other animal products.*

We use *in addition to* to add information to the subject, or to join two or more pieces of information together. *In addition to* can be at the start of or within a sentence.

Examples: *People choose to be vegan for health, environmental and/or ethical reasons.*

People choose to be vegan for health reasons, in addition to environmental and/or ethical reasons.

People who choose to be vegan do so for environmental and/or ethical reasons, in addition to health reasons.

Rewrite the following information using *in addition to*:

a A healthy and varied vegan diet includes fruits, vegetables and plenty of leafy greens, as well as wholegrain products, nuts, seeds and legumes.

b Vegan diets are free of cholesterol and are generally low in fat.

c Calcium is found in dark-green vegetables and many other foods commonly eaten by vegans.

d *Simply Vegan* contains a complete discussion of vegan nutrition plus 160 quick and easy recipes.

VOCABULARY BOX

diet

This word originates from the Greek word *diaita* and the Latin word *dieta*, meaning 'a way or method of living'. As the word became more widely used during the days of the Roman Empire, and later by the French, the meaning became more specific. The word was used to mean 'regular food' as long ago as 1225, and the phrase *put someone on a diet* dates from about 1440. Diet Coke is less than 50 years old (1963).

restaurant

This word comes from the French *restaurer*, meaning 'to restore'. A restaurant was originally a public dining room, and originated in France during the Napoleonic age (early 19th century).

statistics

This German word (*statistik*) was first used in 1770 to refer to the science dealing with data about the condition of a state or community. The meaning 'numerical data collected and classified' is from 1829, and the abbreviated form *stats* was first recorded in 1961. The word *statistician* is from 1825.

vegan

This word was first used in 1944, and comes from *vegetable*. It is used to distinguish people who refuse to eat **all** animal products (eggs, cheese, yoghurt, and so on, as well as meat) from those who only refuse to eat the animals (vegetarians).

Unit 4:
Focus on listening skills

Exam Questions 1–6

 ## Vocabulary

1   Here are some types of transport. Unjumble the letters and then copy and complete the table, writing each type of transport in either the Air, Land or Sea column.

arc   chaty   cleycib   forthvreac   hacoc
lepan   nalobol   reyrf   torcileeph

Air	Land	Sea

2   Choose one type of transport from each column. Then say what you think are the advantages and disadvantages for each one.

 ## Reading

3   You are going to read an Internet article on page **24** about how advertising can have an effect on young people. There are five sections in the article. Each section has a heading:

(a) Children's understanding of advertising
(b) Media literacy
(c) Benefits of advertising to children
(d) Advertising does not encourage children to ask for more
(e) Advertising does not influence diet

In which of the five sections do you think you are more likely to find the following **nine** phrases? Try to give reasons for your choices.

i   ... they comprehend that advertising is there to sell to them.
ii   Advertisements also must not encourage eating or drinking near bedtime.

iii Banning advertising during children's programming would not insulate children from commercial messages ... .

iv By the age of seven or eight, most children are fully aware of the persuasive nature of advertising ... .

v Children have always asked their parents for things ... .

vi Advertising of snack foods directed at children is much greater than that of fruit and vegetables.

vii Children have to develop the ability to make critical comparisons ... .

viii Further restrictions on advertising would affect the choice and quality of programming for children ... .

ix If advertising was banned or restricted, commercial broadcasters would reduce or cease their investment in original programme production.

4 Read the article and find words which have a similar meaning to the following. Write them down. Use your dictionary to help you.

a effect (section **a**)
b purpose (**a**)
c convincing (**a**)
d buyers (**a**)
e protect (**b**)
f connection (**c**)
g income (**c**)
h spending (**c**)
i stopped (**c**)
j large (**c**)
k asking repeatedly (**d**)
l pressure (**e**)
m very clear (**e**)

5 Think about what you have just read and decide whether the following statements are true or false.

a Children do not understand the difference between advertising and normal programme content at an early age.

b Before children start to buy things, they understand the real purpose of advertising is to make them spend money.

c Stopping advertising during children's programmes would not protect them from advertisers' messages.

d Restrictions on advertising would improve the quality of children's programmes.

e Most parents do not believe that television advertising affects their children.

f There is more advertising of fruit and vegetables than snack foods.

g Children take part in less physical activity than they did ten years ago.

h Problems with weight are a result of too many snack foods rather than not enough physical exercise.

Children and advertising

(a) Children's understanding of advertising

Children enjoy and remember advertisements but this does not necessarily mean that they have an impact on their behaviour. Research conducted by Dr Brian Young has shown that children do understand the difference between advertising and editorial or programme content from the age of three. From around the age of five, children also begin to understand the commercial intent of advertising – i.e. that it is trying to sell you something. By the age of seven or eight, most children are fully aware of the persuasive nature of advertising and have an understanding of it. Full understanding increases with age but, before they are acting independently as purchasers, they comprehend that advertising is there to sell to them.

(b) Media literacy

Children today are exposed to a wider range of influences, cultures and media than any other generation. Banning advertising during children's programming would not insulate children from commercial messages. They would still see products they like advertised in a positive light in shop windows – should this also be restricted?

Understanding the role of advertising and marketing is an essential part of growing up and becoming a citizen in a free-market democracy. Children have to develop the ability to make critical comparisons and informed decisions.

(c) Benefits of advertising to children

With worries about safety outside, children's play increasingly takes place within the home. Computer games, television and the Internet are today the main sources of children's entertainment. Further restrictions on advertising would affect the choice and quality of programming for children, forcing them to watch programmes intended for adults instead.

There is a direct correlation between advertising revenue generated during children's programme hours and expenditure on children's programming. If advertising was banned or restricted, commercial broadcasters would reduce or cease their investment in original programme production. This has happened in Sweden, where commercial broadcasters do not exceed five hours a week of children's programming. It is also borne out in Greece, where a ban on toy advertising since 1994 has led to a 40% decline in children's programme investment. Some children-only channels would cease to exist at all. Thus there would be a substantial reduction in the choice and quality of programmes and television channels available to children.

(d) Advertising does not encourage children to ask for more

In research carried out in 1999, only 14% of parents cited television advertising as one of the top five influences on their children. Other research conducted in the same year in Sweden found that, despite a ban on all TV advertising to under-twelve-year-olds, more Swedish adults felt that pestering was a problem (9%) compared with Spanish adults (7%). Children have always asked their parents for things, but laws do not permit advertisements to encourage this.

(e) Advertising does not influence diet

Advertising of snack foods directed at children is much greater than that of fruit and vegetables. Some groups claim this relationship becomes reflected in children's diets, causing diet-related problems.

However, being overweight is a result of the imbalance between energy in and energy out. Whereas foods with high-calorie content have fallen in the last decade, levels of physical activity among children have declined further. For example, since 1986, the number of walking trips made by young people has fallen by 17% for those aged between five and ten years and by 29% for those aged eleven to fifteen years. Problems of overweight are likely to be a product of falling levels of exercise.

Major influences on children's diets do not include advertising, particularly among younger children, who do not make their own purchasing or dietary decisions. In *Recent Research into Children's Dietary Choices* (1994), Dr Peter Stratton found that advertising is not considered a major influence on children's diets, and parents do not believe that it has encouraged children to pester adults for specific foods. He quantified TV advertising as influencing only 5% of food choices and ninth on the list of influences, after family and friends.

Laws about advertising practice are explicit about not encouraging children to eat frequently throughout the day or replace meals with snacks. Advertisements also must not encourage eating or drinking near bedtime.

Adapted from www.fau.org.uk, 1 February 2004.

Research

6 The text you have just read is about advertising and its influence on children. Find **three or four** examples of different advertisements that you like and dislike, and be prepared to tell your class why.

7 What does the law say about children and advertising in your country? Find out as much information as you can.

 Listening

Track 1

8 You are going to listen to a spokesperson from the FAU (Food Advertising Unit) being interviewed about the effects of advertising on children. Before you listen, look at some of the questions which the interviewer asks the spokesperson. What do you think the answers might be?

   a *What do parents and adults think about advertising to children?*
   b *I understand some research has been carried out to determine what parents think about this. What does the research tell us?*
   c *Do parents want stricter controls over advertising aimed at children?*
   d *Do parents and adults see advertising to children as a major problem?*
   e *Does advertising have any effect on diet-related problems?*
   f *Is there any scientific evidence of the extent of advertising's influence on food choice?*

9 Now look at some possible responses to the questions and decide which response could match each question.

   i *Most certainly, although it is difficult to come to any conclusions because the facts seem to contradict themselves.*
   ii *Norway and Belgium have three or four times fewer food advertisements per hour on average than Germany, Denmark, Finland and the Netherlands, yet suffer from higher levels of obesity.*
   iii *Parents see no need for additional rules or laws regarding advertising.*
   iv *Some parents believe that advertising manipulates their children into wanting things they don't need.*
   v *According to a report on the Promotion of Food to Children, published in 2001, there is actually little public concern over food advertising.*
   vi *There is general agreement that advertising is not one of the major influences on children.*

10 Listen to the interview and copy and complete the sentences below.

   a Some parents believe advertising makes their children want things they don't need, whilst others believe advertising helps them to ...... their children will like.
   b Children understand that TV commercials make them want products – this understanding is clear, even amongst the ...... , the youngest children in the group discussions.
   c In a study in 2000, commissioned by the Advertising Education Forum, ... did not mention TV advertising as one of the five major influences on their choice of food.

d In the UK, only five per cent mentioned advertising as an influence and, in Denmark, 41 per cent. In Sweden, where ...... , eleven per cent of parents felt it to be a major influence.

e There is general agreement that advertising is not ...... on children and that, broadly, parents, brothers and sisters, friends and school are more powerful.

f Norway and Belgium have ...... times fewer food advertisements per hour on average than Germany, Denmark, Finland and the Netherlands.

g There is no reason to assume that advertising will ...... affect a child's dietary health. It can influence it, but this influence could just as easily be positive as negative.

h Restricting advertising during children's programming would not protect them from commercial messages. Understanding the role of marketing and developing the ability to make ...... are an essential part of growing up and becoming a citizen in a free-market democracy.

 ## Writing

11 Your school is having a writing competition. The title of the competition is 'What makes a good, safe advertisement?' Write your entry for the competition, expressing your opinion about children and advertising. Use the ideas in this unit to help you. Your entry should be about 150–200 words long (Extended) or 100–150 words long (Core).

 ## Language

12 The words *contradict* and *conclusion* are used in the interview. Each word begins with a different prefix: *contra-* and *con-*. What do these prefixes mean? Use your dictionary to help you.

13 Here are some other prefixes used in this unit. Match them to their meaning. Use your dictionary to help you.

in-	thoroughly, very; through
ex-	shows a negative, an opposite; in, on
en-	under
pro-	former and still living; out, from
per-	in favour of
ad-	to cause to become; make
sub-	in the direction of; towards, to

14 Now find words from the 'Children and advertising' text that begin with the prefixes in the first column of this table:

Prefix	Words from text	Your words
con-	conclusion	conduct, convey
contra-	contradict	contraband, contrast
in-		
ex-		
en-		
pro-		
per-		
ad-		
sub-		

15 You learned from the text that one advantage of advertising to children is that: *it increases the quantity of children's programmes.*

A disadvantage of advertising to children is that: *it could encourage children to eat more snack food.*

Now write one advantage and one disadvantage for each of the following statements. Use some of the advantages and disadvantages phrases you thought of in Unit **3** Exercise **15** of this Workbook.

a Children normally have to go to school until the age of 16.
b Teenagers are normally not allowed to work full-time until they are 16.
c The year is divided into four seasons: autumn, winter, spring and summer.
d More and more families have a computer in their home.
e Children have to do sports at school.

16 Copy and complete this table. All the words have been taken from this unit. You may not be able to fill all the gaps. Use your dictionary to help you.

Adjective	Noun	Adverb	Verb
	children		
			encourage
			develop
	comprehension		
	advertisement		
	product		
			decide
aware			

17 In the box there are twelve words taken from the text in this workbook. Match each word with its antonym in the list below.

negative   fully   persuasive   wider   informed   direct
substantial   major   general   youngest   restrict   useful

a positive
b partially
c minor
d oldest
e useless
f dissuasive
g narrower
h misinformed
i indirect
j small
k specific
l broaden

18 Choose **eight** words from Exercise 17 and use them to write meaningful sentences.

Example: *Her school report was very positive about her improvement in English.*

 VOCABULARY BOX

ability
As long ago as 1380, the word *ablete* was used in France to mean 'expert at doing something'. It was based on the Latin word *habilis*, meaning 'handy' or 'easy to manage'.

advert
This word comes from the French word *avertir*, which means 'to warn'. This was originally a Latin word, *advertere*, meaning 'to turn towards'. Commercial messages (advertisements) have been found from as far back as the time of Pompeii, Italy (nearly 2,000 years ago!).

contradict
This comes from a Latin word, *contradicere*, meaning 'speak against', and was first used in about 1382. The word is made from the preposition *contra-* ('against') and the verb *dicere* ('to speak').

persuade
This word means 'to make someone believe something' and comes from the Latin word *persuadere*, from *per-* ('strongly') + *suadere* ('to urge'). The word can first be found in 1513.

Unit 5:
Exam practice

In this unit, you will have more opportunity to do some examination practice with exam-practice questions which focus on some of the exercises covered in the previous four units: exam Exercises 1 and 2 (reading) and 6 (writing), and listening.

 ## Reading: Exam Exercise 2 (Core)

Read the newspaper article below and then answer the questions which follow.

Computer games health hazards

Doctors are becoming increasingly concerned about the health of children who spend hour after hour glued to computer games. The experts say that young people are exposing themselves to a range of potential hazards, from 'mouse elbow' to 'joystick digit'.

As many as 20 per cent of children have some kind of health problem associated with the overuse of computer games, a recent survey has shown. One in seven children spend so much time in front of video screens that they have black rings around their eyes because of lack of sleep, say the doctors, who interviewed over 1,100 children aged six to eleven and their parents. One in five children showed evidence of stiff muscles in their back and shoulders, a result of the strain from the constant use of a computer mouse or video-game joystick.

This study is the most recent in a series of reports which link health problems with excessive use of video and computer games. All the problems result from repetitive movements and sleep deprivation, and some experts predict that overuse of games could cause long-term heart damage.

'Mouse elbow' is the result of damage to the forearm and elbow. The elbow can also suffer trauma injury if the mouse is moved too vigorously. 'Video eyes' are caused by too little sleep. 'Joystick digit' is a consequence of overuse of the finger on the joystick. 'Vibration finger' is caused by excessive use of computer-game controllers which vibrate. 'Nerve trap' is the result of the neck and head being in the same position for too long.

a What has caused doctors to become concerned about the health of children? [1]

b What percentage of children have a health problem, according to the survey? [1]

c Why do one in seven children have black rings around their eyes? [1]

d How many children and parents were interviewed for the research? [1]

e How old were the children who were interviewed? [1]

f What **two** things do doctors say that the health problems result from? [2]

g How could the heart be damaged? [1]

h List the **five** specific problems identified in the research. [2]

[Total: 10]

 ## Writing: Exam Exercise 6

'Save our playing field' campaign!

The playing field next to our school is the only place nearby where we can play sports. In the summer, the field is also used for festivals and the popular 'world music' concert. Now it is to be sold to a developer so that a new shopping centre can be built! Don't let this happen! Write to your local newspaper expressing your opinions about the importance of the playing field.

Find out more: www.noshops.eur

You have read the above announcement on posters in your town. Write a letter to your friend:

- giving reasons why the playing field should be saved
- saying why your community needs the playing field
- giving alternative suggestions for the site of the new shopping centre.

Your letter should be about 150–200 words long (Extended) or 100–150 words long (Core).

Reading: Exam Exercise 1 (Extended)

Welcome!

Welcome to the new Achileas Sports Centre and Swimming Pool Complex monthly newsletter! We offer a wide variety of activities for you and all your family and friends. Whether your interest is fitness, football, tennis, basketball or swimming, we can offer you an excellent range of activities to suit all your needs. We hope you will enjoy your visit to the new Achileas complex and take advantage of the many facilities available.

Opening hours

Swimming Pool
Monday–Friday	07.00–22.00
Saturday–Sunday & public holidays	08.00–21.00

Sports Centre
Monday–Friday	06.00–22.00
Saturday–Sunday & public holidays	09.00–20.00

Achileas Restaurant
Monday–Saturday	12.00–15.00 & 19.00–23.00
Sunday & public holidays	12.00–15.00 only

Membership

	Children (6–18)	Adults (18+)	Couples (2 adults)	Family (2 adults + 2 children)
Annual	£100	£200	£150 each	£450
6-monthly	£70	£120	£105 each	£255
3-monthly	£50	£75	£65 each	£195
Monthly	£25	£45	£40 each	£120
Weekly	£15	£35	£30 each	£90
Daily	£4	£8	£6	£14

Facilities

Five fitness & special-focus gyms, one children's gym, Olympic pool and children's starter pool, four squash courts, four badminton courts, two basketball courts, eight outdoor tennis courts, two all-weather football pitches, Achileas Sports Shop, Achileas Restaurant.

Focus on gyms

Whatever your fitness level, whatever your age and whatever your goals, we have something to offer you in one of our special-focus gyms! If you would like to lose weight, tone up, increase your strength or improve your health, we have highly qualified staff on hand to motivate you in one of our 'focus' gyms.

Whether you wish to work out once a week or every day, for ten minutes or an hour, after an initial consultation our staff will design your own personal-fitness programme, tailored to suit your individual needs. You will also benefit from regular reviews, where your progress will be monitored and your programme updated or adjusted accordingly.

All of this takes place in one of our five focus gyms: cardiovascular, resistance training, free weights, general and sports injury.

All of our focus gyms offer state-of-the-art machines and excellent user-friendly equipment, catering for all your health and fitness needs.

a What time does the sports centre close on public holidays? **[1]**
b What is the cost for a family for a six-month membership? **[1]**
c How many swimming pools are there? **[1]**
d What non-sport facility does the complex offer? **[1]**
e What do you need to do before the staff can design your
   personal fitness programme? **[1]**
f How is your progress assessed? **[1]**
g What two things do all of the 'focus' gyms offer? **[2]**

[Total: 8]

Track 2

Listening

Listen to the interview about dangers in the home, and complete the notes below. You will hear the interview twice.

Dangers in the home

a Safety is perhaps the most important ...... that young children
   need to learn. **[1]**
b Most accidents occur in the living room, bedroom, kitchen and .... **[1]**
c ...... account for the greatest number. **[1]**
d Medicines should be ...... and out of reach. **[1]**
e Dangers of electricity:
   • overloading powerpoints
   • not checking .... **[1]**
f ...... cause a lot of accidents. **[1]**
g Children must learn that ...... and ...... are not toys. **[1]**
h Two other dangers in the home: ...... and .... **[1]**
i After 30 minutes, a hot drink can still .... **[1]**

[Total: 9]

Unit 6:
Focus on reading skills

Exam Exercise 2

 Vocabulary

1   In Unit **6** of your Coursebook, you talked about the services a language
    school could offer, such as careers guidance. How many others can you
    remember? Make a list.

2   The following eight words appear in the 'Changing schools' text on
    page **47** of your Coursebook. Copy the table and complete as many of the
    gaps as you can.

Noun	Verb	Adjective	Adverb
	discover		
environment			
problem			
education			
communication			
		prepared	
continuation			
independence			

 Reading 1

3   You are going to read a text on page **34** about parents educating their
    children at home instead of sending them to school. Before you look at
    the text, read these questions and make some notes.

    a What do you think the benefits of being educated at home might be?
       Think about parents as well as children.
    b What different experiences do you think a child might have learning
       away from a school environment?

4   Before you write a summary, you first need to find the key points in a
    passage. The next few questions will help you. Read the text 'I want to
    educate my children at home' on page **34**. Then look at the following
    sentences and decide which ones are true, based on what you have read.

a Parents are natural teachers from their child's birth.
b Children need their parents to teach them.
c School improves the natural ability of the child to learn.
d Schools have only existed since recent times.
e Schools become a negative struggle for many children.
f Home-schooling has proved to be beneficial to the child's academic standards.
g Socialisation is achieved by putting children into organised groups.
h Children who choose their own groups to mix in grow into confident adults.

5   Write out the sentences from Exercise **4** which you think are correct.

6   Answer these questions.

a Who plays a more important role in a child's development, according to the writer?
b Why does the writer think that schools interrupt the 'natural flow of learning'?
c When do parents usually start to think about home-schooling for their children?
d What sort of 'little people' are schools seen to produce?
e What does the writer say are the benefits of home-schooling?
f Which negative aspects of school socialisation does the author identify?

I want to educate my children at home

From the day your child was born, you have been home-educating – assisting them in their quest for knowledge of the world around them, answering their questions, teaching them to walk and talk. You have already done the hard stuff, and without a curriculum. In fact, if you truthfully look back at this stage, you yourself have not had much of a hand in all the wonderful things your child has accomplished. Our children are born with the ability to teach themselves everything they need to know about surviving in the world they live in, and they do it well. School interrupts this natural flow of learning and eventually kills it. If you leave children alone and just provide lots of resources, encouragement and a caring environment, that is all they will ever need. Trust them and they will get the job done.

Home-school is an option open to families in Australia, and often the decision to home-educate your child is made well after your child has started school. Schools are a fairly recent invention as they have only been around for about 150 years or so. Before that, parents always taught their children at home, and it was a natural part of life. Going to school is not the natural way for a child to learn and many children struggle with the concept of school. As a result, parents often see a change

for the worse in their children. They become unhappy, angry little people, unable to communicate with parents and siblings as they once did.

An Australian lecturer in education, who has been researching home-education for ten years, has found that children who have had structured lessons at home, as well as children who have had absolutely no structure at home, have turned out to be both socially and academically ahead of schooled peers. The only drawback that he found in the ten years of study was the lost wages of one parent.

Children do not need to be placed in artificial situations so that they can 'become socialised'. Socialisation forced upon children in schools and playgroups is not true socialisation. Real socialisation happens all the time, every minute of the day, with parents, siblings, shopkeepers, in the park and, best of all, children with themselves and their dreams. It happens all the time and we do not need to set it up. The type of socialisation that does happen in the playground is not the type most of us want for our children (the bullying and the peer pressure and the bad language) and children that grow up in charge of their own socialisation grow strong and confident and able to communicate with a wide range of people.

Adapted from 'I have made the decision to home-educate my children', www.home-ed.vic.edu.au, 9 February 2002.

Research

7   Use the Internet to find out as much as you can about home-schooling. Try to get information about the countries it is popular in (apart from Australia), and whether there are organisations which help parents and their children. Is it possible to find out why parents home-educate their children in these countries?

8   In some countries, children are educated at home but by teachers using the Internet and video links – 'virtual teaching'. Find out as much as you can about this method of education.

 ## Writing 1

9   Write a letter to a friend summarising the methods of education you have read about and researched in this unit: home-schooling and virtual teaching. Your letter should be about 150–200 words long (Extended) or 100–150 words long (Core).

 ## Reading 2

10 The following words and phrases appear in the text you are going to read on page 36. Match them to the correct definition. Use your dictionary to help you.

> *contribute   short   salary   graduate   academic   reputation*
> *initially   depend   expenses*

a   connected to education
b   money you earn
c   not enough
d   costs
e   to begin with
f   add
g   good name
h   person who has a university degree
i   rely

11 Find the vocabulary from Exercise 10 in the text.

12 The title of the text you are about to read is 'I was concerned I would be left out'. What do you think the speaker meant by 'left out' here?

a   left out = on my own
b   left out = left alone
c   left out = not included in a group

13 Skim the text (page 36) and check whether your answer to Exercise 12 is correct.

14 Read the text, then copy and complete these sentences.

    a Bimla knew she wanted to go to university ....
    b Although she had been told she'd do well at university ....
    c Bimla thinks that university is for ....
    d Bimla's parents expected her to ....
    e Bimla worked ....
    f The university had ....
    g She needn't have been afraid ....
    h She wants to tell other families ....

I was concerned I would be left out

Bimla always knew that she wanted to go to university when she got her IGCSE results. But she had been worried that she would not be accepted by the other students once she got there. Although she had always been told at her school that she would do well at university, she nonetheless believed that other students would be better than her. 'I know I got good grades at school, but I thought that they wouldn't be enough and that I would be left out by the other students,' she admits. Some of her friends thought she shouldn't even think about going to university but she didn't agree with that and said, 'I think university should be for everyone, no matter where they come from or what their background is.'

Growing up in a large family, she'd always understood that her parents would depend on the children to contribute money to the home. 'We all knew we'd have to help pay the expenses at home, so when I told my parents I wanted to do my IGCSEs before going to university, they weren't very pleased initially,' she recalls. 'But soon they accepted the idea when they thought about the advantages of having a university graduate in the family.'

Money was short at home, so Bimla worked after her IGCSEs and saved nearly everything from her salary. She wanted to work in medicine, so she looked around and found a university near home, which meant she could stay at home and study at the same time.

The university had a good academic reputation and she thought she wouldn't get in, so she was very excited when she was offered a place. 'I never thought it possible,' she admits.

Three years later and she remembers her fears of being left out. 'I've made some really great friends and everybody has been so helpful, even the lecturers! The idea that you are not good enough because you are different is so wrong – university is not like that.'

She wants to say to other families, 'If your child is good enough and really wants to go on to university, then you can't imagine the advantages there will be for you and your family.'

15 Imagine you are someone who was educated the 'home-school' way. You now want to go to university as Bimla did. What do you think would be your strengths and weaknesses at university? Use the table on page 37 to make notes.

	Strengths	Weaknesses
Socialising		
Applying yourself to a structured education		
Dealing with external deadlines and pressures		
Style of work demanded by the university		
Other points		

Writing 2

16 Use the information in the table you completed in Exercise **15** to write a description of what you think your strengths and weaknesses would be at university if you had been home-schooled. Your description should be about 150–200 words long (Extended) or 100–150 words long (Core).

Language

17 These words appear in the text 'I want to educate my children at home' on page **34**. What are their opposites? Two example answers have been provided. Use your dictionary to help you.

born – died
answering – questioning
teaching
hard
wonderful
often

recent
worse
artificial
strong
confident
wide

18 These words have been taken from Unit **6**, but the letters have been jumbled up. Write them out correctly. Use your dictionary to check your spelling. The first letter of each word is given.

Examples: *i i a y b l t* = **a***bility*

n e i o t d u a c = **e***ducation*

a s i t u e v y i r n = **u**......
b s p e u r e s r = **p**......
c r t i t p r n e u = **i**......
d g d p a y r u l n o = **p**......
e d r u s c e t u t r = **s**......

f g s b s i i n l = **s**......
g p c n e t c o = **c**......
h y s a t b u e o l l = **a**......
i t n u a e e o g e c r m n = **e**......
j s s s i i g n a t = **a**......

19 Now match each of the words in Exercise **18** to the correct definition below.

   a brothers and sisters
   b completely
   c a place for advanced learning
   d helping
   e idea
   f a place to play
   g support
   h organised
   i to stop someone or something
   j demands

20 In the two texts, there are some examples of phrasal verbs.

Examples: *look back* – remember

depend on – trust

Match these other phrasal verbs to the correct meaning. Use your dictionary to help you.

Phrasal verb	Meaning
get off	extinguish
go in for	take part in something
go for	test
point out	get little punishment
try out	call attention to
put out	try to get something

21 Write **six** sentences of your own using the phrasal verbs from Exercise **20**.

 VOCABULARY BOX

academy
This word comes from the 15th-century Latin word *academia* and the Greek *Akademeia*. *Akademeia* was a place near Athens, named after the legendary Akademos, who fought in the Trojan Wars. When Plato taught his students on this land, the word *Akademeia* began to mean a 'school' or 'training place'.

learn
From about 1200 until the early 19th century, it was correct in English to say, 'He learned me how to read', but do not use it now! *Leornian* was an old English word meaning 'to get knowledge from'.

ostracise
The ancient Greeks held elections to decide whether someone was an undesirable citizen. Votes were written on pieces of broken pottery (*ostrakon*). People voted undesirable were sent away, or *ostracised*.

school
Old English *scol*, Latin *schola* and Greek *skhole* originally had connections with leisure and spare time! These meanings changed over time to 'a place for discussion', and today the French (*école*), Spanish (*escuela*) and Italian (*scuola*), as well as German (*Schule*), Swedish (*skola*), Welsh (*ysgol*) and Russian (*shkola*) words for school are all very similar.

Unit 7:
Focus on reading and writing skills

Exam Exercise 4

 ## Vocabulary

1   Here are seven jobs from Unit **7** in your Coursebook, but the letters have been jumbled up. What are they? Rewrite them correctly.

>   anatorust   dragreen   heatcre   tenarpcer
>   tilop   torcod   uncanttoac

2   Use these words from the Clayton Anderson interview on page **55** of your Coursebook to complete the sentences.

>   *ample   claustrophobia   gravity   massive   orbit   spectacular*

a   *Surprisingly, I have had no feelings of ....*
b   *It is an ...... amount of space and you can find places for privacy.*
c   *Being a small part of such a ...... project is quite a thrill for me.*
d   *The views of space I experienced were absolutely ....*
e   *When we reached ...... and zero ...... on STS-117, I was ready to go to work!*

 ## Reading 1

3   Skim the 'Have a nice mouth' article (page **40**). Match each paragraph with a subject from the list below.

a   bad breath
b   vitamin C foods
c   gum disease
d   gum inflammation
e   smoking
f   Xylitol sweetener

4   Find these words in the text. What do you think they mean? Use your dictionary to help you.

a   *oral* (paragraph **1**)   **g**   *inflammation* (**3**)
b   *decay* (**1**)   **h**   *susceptible* (**3**)
c   *rinses* (**2**)   **i**   *heal* (**3**)
d   *hailed* (**2**)   **j**   *misconceptions* (**4**)
e   *suppresses* (**2**)   **k**   *advocates* (**4**)
f   *inhibits* (**2**)   **l**   *constricting* (**5**)

5   Look at the article again. Pick out what you think are the important pieces of information in each paragraph.

6   You are going to give a talk about oral hygiene to a group of students at your school. You have decided to use information from this article in your talk. To help plan your talk, read the article, then make two short notes under each of the following headings:

a   The basics of gum and oral health
c   The causes of bad breath
b   Facts about Xylitol
d   Sources of vitamin C and calcium

Have a nice mouth

(1) Periodontal, or gum, disease affects 95 per cent of people, making it the most common of all diseases. It is also the leading cause of tooth loss in adults. Most people are aware of the basics of dental and oral health: twice-daily toothbrushing and regular flossing, dental checks and visits to the hygienist are essential, along with a low-sugar intake. But there are other easy steps to reduce the risk of tooth decay, bleeding gums and bad breath.

(2) Plaque builds up as a mixture of mouth bacteria and food particles in a solution of mucus. A sweetener, Xylitol, which is finding its way into many chewing gums, mouth rinses and toothpastes, is being hailed as the latest effective anti-plaque weapon. Dr Ronnie Levine of the Health Development Agency says: 'As an anti-plaque and anti-caries (tooth decay) agent, Xylitol is possibly the most promising development since the introduction of fluoride.' Xylitol is a bulk sweetener, related to sugar and extracted from birch wood. Unlike most other sugars, Xylitol cannot be converted to acid in the mouth by bacteria. It suppresses unfavourable mouth bacteria and inhibits plaque formation. A recent study showed that the children of mothers who regularly chewed Xylitol-sweetened gum had a 70-per-cent reduction in tooth decay. Sugar-free gums are also a good way of encouraging saliva flow for those who suffer from xerostomia, or dry mouth.

(3) The first sign of periodontal disease is inflammation of the gums, or gingivitis, which develops in pockets between the gum and bone as it progresses. One natural compound showing promise in dealing with this is hyaluronic acid, which is found naturally in the gum and the eye. It has been used to treat eyes after surgery; now it is being used for gum health. Research is in its early stages, but Dr Peter Galgut, a specialist in periodontics, has been using it for about 18 months to control pockets of inflammation. 'It gives significant advantage for promoting healing of gingival pockets in susceptible people, as well as helping to heal mouth ulcers and a type of oral eczema,' he says.

(4) Halitosis (bad breath) plagues many people. Dr Phil Stemmer, founder of the Fresh Breath Centre, says there are two main misconceptions about bad breath: 'The first is that it comes from the stomach, which is physically impossible unless there is a damaged sphincter at the top of the stomach. The other is that a major cause is sulphurous gases given off by oral bacteria.' Dr Stemmer advocates that, after brushing and flossing, people use a tongue scraper, which gets rid of food debris coating the tongue and reduces the reserve of bacteria in the mouth. Another unexpected, but logical, suggestion is to brush your teeth before breakfast to get rid of the bacteria, so they are unable to react with the food to create acid. Acids form within seconds of food entering the mouth, and within a minute or two are strong enough to eat away at tooth enamel.

(Continues on page 41 …)

(*... continued*)

(5) Another hazard for oral health is smoking, which, apart from creating a risk of oral cancer, increases gum disease by constricting blood vessels that deliver nutrients to the gums, contributing to bone breakdown and slowing healing of the tissues. One study concluded that smokers had 38 per cent bone loss compared with 9 per cent in non-smokers. Smokers need to take extra vitamin C for gum health, as smoking destroys this nutrient.

(6) Some nutrients are important for oral health, and bleeding gums can be an early sign of scurvy, caused by a deficiency or lack of vitamin C. Trials have shown that eating more foods rich in vitamin C, such as citrus and kiwi fruit, strawberries, broccoli and cabbage, can reverse vitamin-C-related bleeding gums. While it may sound obvious advice, calcium has been linked in several studies to increased periodontal disease, and it is important to make sure that you get at least 700 mg of calcium daily in your diet, from foods such as yoghurt, cheese, green leafy vegetables, nuts, seeds, tinned sardines or salmon, and bread.

Adapted from an article by Suzannah Oliver in *The Times*, 28 August 2001.

Research

7 There are several technical and scientific words in the article. Find and copy them, and then find out what they are in your own language using a bilingual dictionary.

8 How can you become a dentist? What do you have to study? How long does it take? Use the Internet to find out.

Writing 1

9 Use your notes from Exercise **6** to write your talk. It should be about 150–200 words long (Extended) or 100–150 words long (Core).

Reading 2

10 There is a programme on television called *Dirty Jobs*. What do you think the programme is about? Have you ever seen an episode from the series? Who is the host of the show? Discuss it with your friends.

11 Find words in the text 'Dirty Jobs' (page **42**) which have similar meanings to the following words and phrases. Note them down.

a presenter (paragraph 1)
b jobs (1)
c with (1)
d test (1)
e combination (2)
f humour (2)
g dangers (3)

h a result of (4)
i very visual (4)
j received large numbers of (4)
k paid for (4)
l idea (4)
m advertisements for the programme (4)

12 Read the text in more detail and copy and complete the notes below.

> ### Dirty jobs
>
> Programme name (**a**) ...... on (**b**) ...... Channel.
>
> Show started in (**c**) ...... and series began (**d**) ...... months later.
>
> Different programme versions shown in Europe, (**e**) ...... and (**f**) ....
>
> Three things which are appealing about the show: the presenter, (**g**) ...... and (**h**) ....
>
> Rowe works alongside other workers doing things which are uncomfortable, (**i**) ...... or (**j**) ....
>
> Originally, show called (**k**) ....

Dirty jobs

(1) *Dirty Jobs* is a programme on the Discovery Channel in which the host, Mike Rowe, is shown performing difficult, strange and/or messy occupational duties alongside professional workers. The show started with three pilot episodes in November 2003, and returned as a series on 26 July 2005. The episodes shown on the European Discovery Channel sometimes include scenes that were not included in the US version. An Australian version of the show commenced airing on the Nine Network on 7 October 2007.

(2) The appeal of the show is the juxtaposition of Mike Rowe, a well-spoken man of television with a sharp, sarcastic wit, the situations in which he's put and the colourful personalities of the men and women who actually do that job for a living.

(3) A worker takes on Rowe as a fully involved assistant during a typical day at work, during which he works hard to complete every task as best he can despite discomfort, hazards or situations that are just plain disgusting. The 'dirty job' often includes cameraman Doug Glover getting just as dirty as Rowe.

(4) The show is a spin-off from a local San Francisco programme called *Somebody's Gotta Do It* that host Mike Rowe once did. After completing a graphic piece on cows and dairy farming, Rowe was inundated with letters expressing 'shock, horror, fascination, disbelief and wonder'. Rowe then sent the tape to the Discovery Channel, who commissioned a series based on this concept. *Dirty Jobs* is now produced by Craig Piligian (Executive Producer) of Pilgrim Film & Television. The Discovery Channel Executive Producer is Gena McCarthy. Mike has stated in recent promos that he originally wanted to honour his father, a lifetime pig farmer, by bringing fame to the less-than-glorious careers.

Adapted from en.wikipedia.org, 13 January 2008.

 ## Writing 2

13 Use the notes in Exercise **12** to write a summary of the information in the text. Do not write more than about 80 words.

Language

14 In Unit **7** of the Coursebook, these **relative pronouns** were used:

> *A carpenter is someone who makes things from wood.*
>
> *The kit consists of four straps which attach to your trampoline and to stakes in the ground.*

Now write complete sentences using the correct relative pronoun (some pronouns will have to be used more than once).

a	There is a film on at the cinema		people play tennis.
b	A fireman is a person		they got married?
c	Is this the article in the newspaper	who	I would like to see.
d	Do you know the reason	which	it was valued more than it is now.
e	Do you think they would forget the day	that where	is a small island.
f	A cathedral is a place	when	passed all her exams.
g	That was the girl		talks about the best hotels?
h	The carpenter is from a place	why	loves his job.
i	Their craft is from a time		they went on strike?
j	Wimbledon is a club		is usually quiet and peaceful.

15 In the Coursebook, the words *assembling* and *professional* appear.

Use the table below to make more words which are spelt with *-ss-*.

Example: *assertion*

a	a		ive
b	a		ue
c	ba		ette
d	pa		ertion
e	ca	ss	oon
f	me		ive
g	ma		port
h	ti		ume
i	succe		age
j	pa		ful

16 Match the words from Exercise 15 to a definition below:

Example: *to think something is true – assume*

a paper handkerchief
b very large
c opposite of active
d something you strongly believe
e official document you must travel with
f to think something is true
g doing well
h magnetic tape
i information given to someone
j large woodwind instrument

17 Look at the passage 'An art no more?' on page 51 of your Coursebook and answer the following questions.

a Find five adjectives in the first paragraph. The first letter is given to you.

Example: *quick-moving*

i w......
ii m......
iii t......
iv a......
v d......

b Find an adjective in paragraph 2. Write down the comparative and superlative forms of that adjective.

Example: *large – larger – largest*

c Find four examples of compound nouns used in the text.

Example: *saw + dust = sawdust*

d Find synonyms for these words in the text.

Example: *assist – help*

i very
ii gentle
iii wood
iv distinctive
v present

 VOCABULARY BOX

carpenter
This comes from the Latin word *carpentarius*, which originally meant a 'wagon- or cart-maker'. Over time, the work of the wagon-maker expanded to involve all things made from wood and so, today, we use the word *carpenter*.

episode
This comes from the Greek word *epeisodion*, meaning 'addition' + 'entrance'. In the 17th century, the word was used to mean an additional event in a story, from where *episode* gets its meaning today of one part in a series.

handkerchief
This is made from two words: *hand* and *kerchief*. *Kerchief* is from an Old French word, *courchief*, which meant 'to cover the head', from *couvrir* ('to cover') and *chief* ('head'). So the modern meaning of the word *handkerchief* is rather strange, when you think about it!

tooth
This word comes from the Old English *toth*. The Latin equivalent is *dens*, which explains why we go to the dentist and not the tooth doctor!

Unit 8:
Focus on writing skills

Exam Exercises 6 and 7

 Vocabulary

1   Look at these words from Unit 8 in your Coursebook. Are they spelt correctly? Discuss them with a classmate. Correct any words which you think are incorrect. Then look in your Coursebook to check.

> advertisment   assosiation   availabel   beleive
> decreesed   dictiunary   increaseingly   literecy
> materiels   secondery   studing

2   Find the twelve words from Exercise 1 in the wordsearch.

S	D	I	C	T	I	O	N	A	R	Y	N	Y
A	E	R	W	M	Z	Q	J	M	R	O	L	S
V	S	C	R	G	P	H	K	K	I	G	L	T
A	T	M	O	F	B	N	V	T	N	A	G	C
I	U	W	P	N	M	M	A	I	I	W	O	D
L	D	T	H	B	D	I	S	R	T	F	V	E
A	Y	N	F	K	C	A	E	T	R	G	E	C
B	I	H	L	O	E	T	R	J	W	V	R	R
L	N	P	S	R	A	G	Z	Y	B	H	N	E
E	G	S	C	M	M	N	Y	L	R	F	M	A
Y	A	N	B	E	L	I	E	V	E	F	E	S
L	I	T	E	R	A	C	Y	L	P	T	N	E
A	D	V	E	R	T	I	S	M	E	N	T	D

 Reading 1

3   You are going to read a newspaper article on page 46 about a disabled man who has a monkey to help him with everyday tasks. Before you read, think about the ways in which a monkey could help a disabled person. Make a list.

4   These words and phrases appear in the text. What do they mean? Use a dictionary to help you.

> *companion   donations   foster parents   furnished   lap   manipulate*
> *paralysed   primates   quadriplegics   raise   trains* (**verb**)

5 Skim the text and check whether any of your ideas from Exercise **3** appear. Do not worry about the gaps at the moment.

6 Read the text again and complete the gaps using the words and phrases from Exercise **4**. Think about what part of speech is required in each gap.

7 Answer the following questions about the text.

    a List three tasks that Minnie can perform for Cook.
    b What other tasks do the monkeys learn to do? List five.
    c Why did Cook have to sell his house?
    d How did Cook hear about Helping Hands?
    e How many staff at the 'college' work with monkeys?
    f How is the third classroom different from the second?
    g What do the monkeys do after their training sessions?

Monkeys lend a 'Helping Hand'

Two little hands changed Craig Cook's life. When he was **(a)** ...... after an accident in 1996, a series of other personal losses followed. He lost his job as a plastics design engineer, a holiday home in Arizona, and then had to sell his two-storey house because it no longer met his needs. Mr Cook, a former high-school athlete, believed he would walk again, but three years later he was still in a wheelchair.

Cook turned to his friends and parents for support. But sometimes that wasn't enough. Then, in 2001, a friend told him about Helping Hands, a 'monkey college' in Boston that **(b)** ...... Capuchin monkeys to assist **(c)** ....

For Cook, the arrival of Minnie meant he no longer had to worry about losing his lifeline – his cell phone. Before, if it slipped off his **(d)** ...... , he'd have to wait for someone to come along. Now, if it falls, he points and says, 'Minnie, fetch.' The monkey also helps him to remove frozen dinners from the freezer and to put them in the microwave. This allows Cook, who can move his arms but not his hands, to make dinner by himself, rather than wait for his night-time nurse.

Minnie's most frequent job is that of **(e)** .... And, for a small monkey, she has a big presence, happily 'talking' as she sits on his shoulder, running her hands through his hair.

(f) ...... **(g)** ...... the monkeys. When an animal's attention span and activity level are appropriate, it moves to the 'college' and spends two years learning to perform various tasks. There, each monkey has its own teacher but it also interacts with other staff members. Of the ten full-time employees at the facility, eight work with the animals.

In their first classrooms, which are very plain, the **(h)** ...... are introduced to key words and tasks, such as bringing an item or turning on a light switch. They also learn to follow a laser pointer, which tells them which objects to **(i)** .... Correct responses are rewarded with the ring of a bell, praise and a taste of juice or cream cheese.

As the monkeys progress, they move to a second classroom, which has cupboards, a wheelchair and a refrigerator-sized cage, like the one that will eventually serve as their bedroom and bathroom.

A third classroom looks like a **(j)** ...... apartment. Here the monkeys master such skills as changing a CD, turning the pages of a book, pouring a water bottle and scratching an itch. They also learn to ride on an electric wheelchair.

(*Continues on page 47 ...*)

(*... continued*)

Formal training sessions last 30 to 60 minutes per day, though the monkeys are out and about during much of the day, practising what they've learned. The cost of training is about $30,500 per monkey, which is paid for by **(k)** .... There are 35 'students' at Helping Hands now. When a monkey is ready to move to its new home, it's accompanied by a placement trainer. The trainer ensures a smooth transition for animal and human.

Adapted from www.csmonitor.com, 2008.

Research

8   Find out as much information as you can about how animals can help humans with special needs. What services are available in your own country? Produce a chart or poster containing all the information you find.

Writing 1

9   Read this exam-type question.

> Your teacher is planning a special weekend trip for you and your classmates. During the weekend you will be able to take part in various activities that you do not normally do at school.
>
> Your teacher wants your ideas for what activities might be offered. S/he has suggested soccer, tennis, kickboxing and karate.
>
> Write a letter to your teacher about the activities you would like to take part in. You can choose from your teacher's ideas, or make your own suggestions.
>
> In your letter, say:
> * what the activity involves
> * why you want to do it
> * why it would be suitable for other members of your class.
>
> Your letter should be about 150–200 words long (Extended) or 100–150 words long (Core).

10 In this particular question, there is quite a lot of information for you to read and understand. In order to make sure you answer the question properly, you should:

a   read the question very carefully
b   put all the words which give you general information in one list
c   put all the words which give you instructions in a second list
d   put all the words which tell you what you have to write about in a third list.

11 Read the sample answer on page **48** and complete the gaps with suitable phrases from the list below.

> I hope that you will   I like the idea of   I think having
> I'd like to play   I'm writing to let you know   I've never done
> My idea is to   we could have   we never have much chance to

Dear Mr Pilot,

(a) ...... which activity I would like to do during our special weekend school trip.

(b) ...... kickboxing before but, as I am afraid of being hurt, I don't think that would be a good activity for me to do! **(c)** ...... soccer but I think that at this time of the year it will be too hot with all that running about. **(d)** ...... tennis but I did that last year with my family.

(e) ...... take our bikes with us and to go for a long ride. At the end of the ride, **(f)** ...... a barbecue or a picnic. Everyone in our class has a suitable bike and here in the town **(g)** ...... ride in the countryside, so I think this would be a wonderful opportunity for all of us. Also, **(h)** ...... a barbecue or picnic when we finish would make us all ride very fast!

(i) ...... consider my suggestion – I can't wait for our weekend trip!

Best wishes,

Alex

(190 words)

12   Answer this exam-practice question:

> You recently went on a weekend activity trip with your classmates. During the weekend, you took part in activities that you do not normally do at school.
>
> Write an article for your school or college magazine in which you describe what activities you took part in.
>
> In your article, you should include the following:
> - where you went and what activities you did
> - what you thought of the activity weekend
> - whether or not you would recommend the activity weekend.
>
> Your article should be about 150–200 words long (Extended) or 100–150 words long (Core).

 Reading 2

13   You are going to read an article written to help students prepare themselves before doing an oral presentation. The writer gives his students the following six guidelines. What information do you think you will read in each section? Make notes.

- Be open to criticism
- Be positive at all times
- Good preparation is a pre-requisite
- Know what to do
- Practise, practise, practise
- Use various materials and aids

14 Quickly skim the text below and match the section headings in Exercise 13 with the information given.

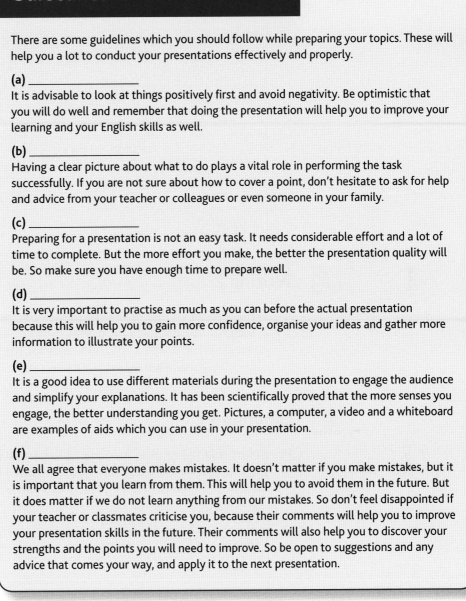

Guidelines

There are some guidelines which you should follow while preparing your topics. These will help you a lot to conduct your presentations effectively and properly.

(a) _____
It is advisable to look at things positively first and avoid negativity. Be optimistic that you will do well and remember that doing the presentation will help you to improve your learning and your English skills as well.

(b) _____
Having a clear picture about what to do plays a vital role in performing the task successfully. If you are not sure about how to cover a point, don't hesitate to ask for help and advice from your teacher or colleagues or even someone in your family.

(c) _____
Preparing for a presentation is not an easy task. It needs considerable effort and a lot of time to complete. But the more effort you make, the better the presentation quality will be. So make sure you have enough time to prepare well.

(d) _____
It is very important to practise as much as you can before the actual presentation because this will help you to gain more confidence, organise your ideas and gather more information to illustrate your points.

(e) _____
It is a good idea to use different materials during the presentation to engage the audience and simplify your explanations. It has been scientifically proved that the more senses you engage, the better understanding you get. Pictures, a computer, a video and a whiteboard are examples of aids which you can use in your presentation.

(f) _____
We all agree that everyone makes mistakes. It doesn't matter if you make mistakes, but it is important that you learn from them. This will help you to avoid them in the future. But it does matter if we do not learn anything from our mistakes. So don't feel disappointed if your teacher or classmates criticise you, because their comments will help you to improve your presentation skills in the future. Their comments will also help you to discover your strengths and the points you will need to improve. So be open to suggestions and any advice that comes your way, and apply it to the next presentation.

Adapted from 'Taking the fear out of presentations' by Ahmed Al-Ajmi, *Youth Observer* (Muscat, Oman), September 2007.

15 What do the following words and phrases mean? Use a dictionary to help you.

  a *optimistic* (paragraph a)
  b *vital* (b)
  c *gain* (d)
  d *gather* (d)
  e *engage* (e)

16 Copy and complete the table below. You may not be able to write a word in all the gaps.

Noun	Verb	Adjective	Adverb
topic			
			effectively
	hesitate		
		considerable	
confidence			
	illustrate		
	attract		
			scientifically
		disappointed	
suggestion			

 ## Writing 2

17 Write a letter to one of the organisations you researched in Exercise **8**, asking for more information about the services it offers, and the prices it charges. Write about 150–200 words for the Extended curriculum or 100–150 words for the Core curriculum.

 ## Language

18 Below and continuing on page **51** are some commonly used British English (BrE) and American English (AmE) words. Copy the table and complete the gaps. Use your dictionary to help you.

BrE	AmE
colour	color
analyse	
travelled	
programme	
cheque	
	labor
	theater
	donut
centre	
metre	
gaol	

	humor
	pajamas
honour	
	catalog
	maneuver
	tire
practise (v) practice (n)	
aeroplane	

19 There are ten words in the wordsearch which have something to do with letter writing, or which you may write in a letter. How many can you find?

F	S	I	G	N	A	T	U	R	E
A	F	X	A	D	D	R	E	S	S
I	O	Y	D	E	A	R	W	X	X
T	R	I	N	F	O	R	M	A	L
H	M	Z	D	L	T	E	Y	L	B
F	A	T	A	H	X	P	O	F	K
U	L	N	T	Q	T	L	U	H	T
L	T	W	E	P	P	Y	R	K	M
L	Z	Y	X	Q	B	Y	S	M	L
Y	S	I	N	C	E	R	E	L	Y

20 In your Coursebook, you will find these words.

> *Internet* – a computer system used to exchange information worldwide
> *electronic language* – specially adapted language to use on electronic equipment

Here are more words. Some are rather strange. Match each one to its correct definition.

buzzy	press the button on a computer mouse
click	a computer file appended to an e-mail
tweenager	a middle-aged person associated with youth culture
retail therapy	lively and exciting
attachment	loose-fitting cotton trousers with large pockets
digital divide	determine the size, shape and form of a written document
mobe	division between those who have and those who don't have computers
adultescent	mobile phone
format	a child between the ages of ten and fourteen
cargo pants	the practice of shopping to make you feel happy

Part 2

21 Copy and complete the following sentences using the words from Exercise **20**.

  a The ...... between rich and poor nations is becoming more obvious as technology improves.
  b She is a real ...... , as dolls are of no interest to her any more. She's outgrown them.
  c Unhappy people often find ...... helps them improve their frame of mind, but then they are left with the bills to pay.
  d There were a lot of older people at the pop concert. They are obviously going through their ...... stage of life.
  e I've received your e-mail but there is no ...... so I haven't got the information I need.
  f The party was great. There was a really ...... atmosphere all night.
  g Just call me on my ...... if you need me.
  h Don't forget to left ...... if you want to highlight something.
  i Remember to ...... all the documents correctly before you hand in your project.
  j These ...... are great and practical for travelling in.

22 Here are **five** more words. Find definitions for them and write a sentence using each word correctly.

  a browser
  b mitch
  c garage (not the car type!)
  d duvet day
  e yah (not hello!)

 VOCABULARY BOX

computer
The verb *compute* comes from the Latin *computare*, meaning 'to count', and was first used in 1631. Not long afterwards (in 1646), the word *computer* came to mean 'a person who does mathematical calculations'. In 1897, the word was introduced for mechanical calculating machines and, in 1945, it was first given to what we today know as a 'programmable digital electronic machine' – that is, a computer!

foster
This comes from an Old English word, *fostrian*, meaning 'to supply with food, support', which in turn comes from the word *fostor*, meaning 'food'. The modern meaning of bringing up a child was first used in the early 13th century.

letter
This comes from the Latin word *littera*, which refers to letters of the alphabet.

quadriplegic
This medical word uses the Latin *quadri-* (meaning 'four') and the Greek *-plegic* (meaning 'to strike'). It means someone paralysed in all four limbs. A correct all-Greek form would be *tessaraplegic*!

Unit 9:
Focus on listening skills

Exam Questions 9 and 10

 ## Vocabulary

1   What headings would you normally find in a CV? Think back to Unit **9** in
    your Coursebook and copy and complete the following:

    E......
    H......
    L......
    P...... i......
    Q......
    R......
    W...... e......

2   In what order would you expect to find the above information in a CV?
    Look back at your Coursebook (pages **156–157**) to check.

 ## Reading

3   Here is the title of an article you are going to read:

    Folk maestro looks back on life in dance

    Which of the descriptions below best matches the title?

    • A person who knows about different types of dance
    • A famous traditional dancer who is now too old to dance
    • A young dancer talking about another famous dancer

4   Scan the text (page **54**) and find these numbers. What do they refer to?

    Example: *98 – age the ex-dancer is at the time of the interview*

a	twelve	**f**	1955
b	1906	**g**	1943
c	1920	**h**	Fifty
d	1937	**i**	four
e	1945		

5 These sentences are based on the article. Decide whether they are true or false.

a Igor Moiseyev no longer goes to work every day.
b He first became a folk dancer at the Bolshoi Theatre.
c His wife, Irini, used to be a dancer.
d All his dancers are guaranteed a place in his dance group.
e His father thought that dance would be important.
f Igor was mainly interested in folk dance.
g He travelled abroad in 1945 to France and Britain.
h The government gives support to his group.
i He thinks that folk dance is as popular as pop music.
j Every year, pupils graduate from the school.

6 Rewrite the false sentences to make them true.

Example: *Igor Moiseyev no longer goes to work every day.*

Igor Moiseyev continues to go to work every day.

Folk maestro looks back on life in dance

Igor Moiseyev has refused to give up work. At the age of 98, the head of Russia's best-known folk-dance group continues to go to work every day and takes part in training dancers.

A small figure in a black cap, Moiseyev has kept the distinguished looks that helped him in his first career as a classical dancer at the Bolshoi Theatre in Moscow.

'I think I'm the only one, not just in dance, but in any area, who works at the age of 98,' says Moiseyev. 'I don't want to retire.' The Artistic Director of both the group and its training school spends several hours each day at work, aided by his younger wife, Irini, who, like the other staff, is one of his former dancers.

'Igor Moiseyev most of all enjoys going to the young children's lessons,' says the Director, Yelena Shcherbakova, of the school, which trains dancers from the age of twelve for a possible place in the group.

Born in Kiev in 1906, Moiseyev first got interested in dance while travelling across the Ukrainian countryside with his aunts, who worked as teachers. In 1920, his father enrolled him in a dance school, hoping that dance would give him the skills that a young man needs. He then moved quickly up the career ladder but his dream was to perform folk dance professionally, and, in 1937, he formed a small company. In 1945, the company became the first Soviet dance group to travel abroad and, in 1955, toured France and Britain, where Moiseyev recalled that the group was particularly enthusiastic about watching 'Scottish dancers in kilts'.

Like the Bolshoi Theatre and other cultural organisations, Moiseyev's dance group receives finance from the government, and it is just as popular today as it was in the past. 'It's enough to come to our concerts and see how many are in the audience and how they receive us,' Moiseyev says.

But there are some differences, Moiseyev admitted. Russian pop music has partly overshadowed the folk heritage. 'I think that for some reason more attention is given to pop, while I cultivated folk music,' he says.

The Moiseyev tradition is set to continue as long as the group's school, founded in 1943, keeps training new generations of dancers. Fifty pupils of both sexes graduate every four years, with the best joining the dance group.

Adapted from www.moscowtimes.ru, 23 January 2004.

Research

7 What traditional folk dances and music do you have in your country? Are there any famous theatres for cultural events? Design and produce a poster informing people about a cultural event or events.

Writing 1

8 Write a letter to your local newspaper telling the Editor about the event or events in Exercise 7. Make sure you include information about the venue, dates, times and prices, plus anything else you think is important. Write about 150–200 words for the Extended curriculum or 100–150 words for the Core curriculum.

Listening

9 You are going to hear an Indian classical dancer talking about her career.

Before you listen, match the words and phrases taken from the interview with a similar word or phrase. Do not worry about the 'Tick' column at the moment.

Word/s from text	Similar words	Tick
classical	experts	
crucial	decision	
debutante	vital	
critics	traditional	
judgement	important	
raved	poor	
prestigious	support	
choreograph	reporters	
irrespective of	with no regard to	
impoverished	newcomer	
connoisseurs	enthused	
promote	compose a dance	

10 Listen to the interview. Tick off the words in Exercise 9 as you hear them.

11   Listen again and match the phrases in columns **A** and **B** below to make meaningful sentences or phrases. This will help you to understand the text.

A	B
a The Arangetram performance	of India.
b A special offering	by the debutante.
c The judgement	group of 60 performers.
d Has the unique distinction	of the critics is crucial.
e To dance at the prestigious	residence of the President.
f Leading dance gurus	children and the poor.
g Different dance forms	is crucial for a dancer
h Enjoys teaching	of making over 1,600 live performances.
i She has her own	such as Indian folk dancing.

Example: *a The Arangetram performance is crucial for a dancer.*

12   Read and answer the following questions. Use the transcript on pages **130–131** to check your answers.

   a How is the performance of the Arangetram important to a new dancer?
   b What response did Dr Jayasinghe receive when she performed the Arangetram?
   c In what way was Dr Jayasinghe different from other dancers who had performed at the President's residence?
   d Name **four** things that Mr Pillai's style of teaching includes.
   e Who does Dr Jayasinghe particularly enjoy teaching?
   f Name **one** social problem in India which Dr Jayasinghe mentions.
   g How long was her solo performance?
   h Name **five** countries she has visited.

 Writing 2

13   Look at Dr Jayasinghe's answers and write down what you remember of the interviewer's questions.

Interviewer: Good evening to our listeners and to our special guest this evening – Dr Sinduri Jayasinghe, the famous Indian classical dancer.

Dr Jayasinghe: Good evening, and thank you for inviting me.

Int'er: Now, Dr Jayasinghe, our listeners are waiting to hear about your career as a professional Indian classical dancer. **(a)** ...... ?

Dr J.:   Well, it all started at the theatre, where I was born.

Int'er: **(b)** ...... ?

Dr J.:   Yes! My mother was actually at the theatre watching a performance when she gave birth to me.

Int'er: **(c)** ...... ?

Dr J.: I started learning classical dance forms that originated in southern India at a very early age. I became famous when I danced the 'Arangetram', which is a very crucial performance for a dancer.

Int'er: **(d)** ...... ?

Dr J.: It is a special offering by the debutante to her teacher, family, friends and critics. The performance can have a great impact on the dancer's career, as the judgement of the critics is crucial. Fortunately, the response was extremely complimentary about me, and I was even raved about by the critics and media alike.

Int'er: **(e)** ...... ?

Dr J.: Well, since then, I have had the unique distinction of making over 1,600 live performances, besides being one of the youngest dancers invited to dance at the prestigious residence of the President of India. Also, I am a graduate from the Madras Music College and I was selected best dancer of Tamil Nadu state in 1984.

Int'er: Tell us something about your training.

Dr J.: Since the age of three, I have had intensive training from Mr Pillai, who is one of the leading dance gurus of India. His style of teaching includes history, theory, dance music, development and dance technique.

Int'er: **(f)** ...... ?

Dr J.: Well, I choreograph all of my own productions, as well as dance programmes for other artists in different dance forms, such as Indian folk dances and many other traditional folk dances of India and Sri Lanka.

Int'er: **(g)** ...... ?

Dr J.: No. I love to teach dance to all those interested, irrespective of their age and ability. I particularly enjoy teaching children and the poor. I have been teaching girls from impoverished homes for free, as my contribution to society.

Int'er: That is wonderful. **(h)** ...... ?

Dr J.: Well, I have been an 'A' grade artist for over ten years in Indian television. My performances have been televised a number of times on the *National Programme of Music and Dance* and on regional programmes. As a young dancer, I proved that I was capable of dancing solo for three hours at a stretch to an audience of dance connoisseurs. Also, I am the lead dancer of my own group of 60 performers. Since 1986, I have toured the United Kingdom, France, Germany, the former Soviet Union, Canada, Singapore, Malaysia, Japan and the USA. Finally, I am an artist for the Indian Council of Cultural Relations of the Indian government, which sends members throughout the world as goodwill ambassadors to promote Indian culture.

Int'er: Well, Dr Jayasinghe, that is certainly an amazing career. I would like to thank you on behalf of myself and our listeners for being with us today.

Part 2

Language

14 Look at these sentences from the article about Igor Moiseyev.

> *Igor Moiseyev has refused to give up work. At the age of 98, the head of Russia's best-known folk-dance group continues to go to work every day and takes part in training dancers.*

> *A small figure in a black cap, Moiseyev has kept the distinguished looks that helped him in his first career as a classical dancer at the Bolshoi Theatre in Moscow.*

Match the verbs in blue with the correct tense from the options below:

present   present perfect   past

When we write about the experiences of a living person, we often need to use these three tenses in order to:

• describe what the person did in the past (e.g. finished events) – *past*
• describe what the person has done during their life (e.g. experiences) – *present perfect*
• describe what the person does now (e.g. habits) – *present*.

15 Read the article on page **54** again. Find as many verbs as you can which occur in the past, present perfect or present tense. For each verb, make sure you identify when the event occurred or occurs.

16 Think about your own life so far. Write a short paragraph (about 100 words) in which you describe what you did in the past (e.g. finished events), the things you have done during your life (e.g. experiences) and what you do now (e.g. habits).

17 Dr Jayasinghe says: *I love to teach dance to all those interested, irrespective of their age and ability.*

Irrespective of here means that age and ability are of no importance.

Use the following pieces of information to write complete sentences using *irrespective of*. You will need to think carefully about what you write.

Example: *repair the damage / cost not important*

We will repair the damage irrespective of the cost.

a win the race / tiredness not important
b complete the puzzle / difficulty not important
c go for a walk / weather not important
d go swimming / temperature of water not important
e visit China / language not a problem

18 Copy and complete the word puzzle by adding these words to the word *choreograph*.

artistic	critics	group	theatre
classical	dance	performance	training
concert	folk	technique	

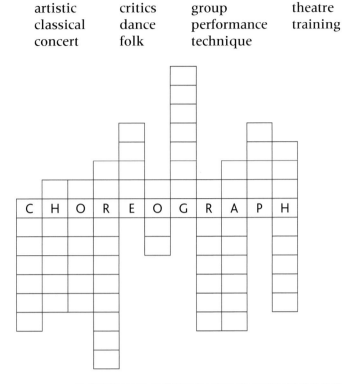

 VOCABULARY BOX

choreograph
First used in the late 18th century in French (*chorégraphie*), this word comes from the Greek *khoreia* ('dance') + *graphein* ('to write').

dance
This word dates back to the 13th century and comes from the Old English *daunces* and originally from the Old French *danser*. The actual origin is uncertain.

theatre
In ancient times, a theatre was an open-air place for viewing spectacles, from the Latin *theatrum* and

Greek *theatron* (*thea* = 'view' + *tron* = 'place'). British spelling changed to –*re* around 1700, while American spelling retained the older –*er* ending.

tradition
First used in about 1300, this word comes from the Old French *tradicion* and Latin *traditionem*, meaning 'deliver', 'surrender', 'hand over'. The word is made from the prefix *trans-*, meaning 'over', and the verb *dare*, meaning 'to give'. The modern meaning is 'handed over, or down, from generation to generation'.

Unit 10:
Exam practice

In this unit, you will have more opportunity to do some examination practice with exam-practice questions which focus on some of the exercises covered in the previous four units: exam Exercises 2 (reading), 3 (reading and writing) and 6 and 7 (writing), and listening.

 ## Reading: Exam Exercise 2 (Core)

The value of cheese ...

Parmesan cheese, without which your plate of spaghetti just does not taste right, has for many years been used as security for loans by banks in the north of Italy. In a vast warehouse near the town of Parma, owned by the Banco Credito Emiliano, there are literally hundreds of thousands of wheels of cheese, each one ripening by the day, and increasing in value as they mature.

The cheeses offer short-term financing for local people until the cheese is ready to sell. Most banks will provide loans of between 65% and 70% of the value of the cheese when it enters the warehouse. A fresh wheel of Parmesan usually weighs about 50 kg but, as it matures, it will lose about 20% (or 10 kg) of its initial weight. However, the more mature a cheese becomes, the greater its value.

24 months old $20–40/ kilo

12 months old $10.50/ kilo

After the first twelve months in the warehouse, Parmesan cheese is worth about $10.50 per kilo, whereas after two years, the price has more than doubled. In some large London stores, two-year-old Parmesan sells for $45 per kilo.

For the banks around Parma, Parmesan cheese has offered a very low security risk for more than 70 years. The process itself is painstaking, and dates back to the 14th century, when Benedictine monks first made the now-world-famous cheese. While the machinery, as well as the financing, has changed over the years, the love and care which goes into the production of Parmesan cheese remains unique. Rows of large copper containers, called vats, steam as warm milk bubbles and froths; the cheese mixture is whipped, heated and then cooled; finally, the soft cheese is placed in a net-like bag, and then into a mould.

But modern technology now provides each wheel of Parmesan with its own personal air-conditioning system, which ensures that the air surrounding it is cooled to 18–20 degrees centigrade, with an air humidity level of 80%. There is even a special room where cheeses which have suffered some type of superficial damage can receive special attention.

Read the article on page **60** and answer the following questions.

a What happens to the value of a wheel of Parmesan as it ripens? **[1]**
b How much does a full-size Parmesan weigh once it has matured? **[1]**
c Who were the first people to make Parmesan cheese? **[1]**
d What happens to the cheese mixture after it has cooled? **[1]**
e What has been the effect of modern technology on the process of
making Parmesan cheese? **[2]**
f Make a list of four pieces of information about the financial value
of Parmesan cheese. **[4]**

[Total: 10]

Reading and writing: Exam Exercise 3 (Extended)

You attend the Instituto Acapulco, 6 San Miguel de Allende, 1022 Mexico
City. Your school's headteacher has informed you that your class will be
attending a Humanities course in Belize. Your Geography teacher at the school
has asked you to research all the information and to complete the application
form for your class.

Information

A total of 28 students (16 girls and 12 boys) will attend the course, accompanied by three teachers. The students will be accommodated in pairs at the course centre. The course itself will last for five days, from Monday 20 June until Friday 24 June. However, because of the long journey, the group will depart from Mexico City on the Saturday before the start of the course and return on Saturday 25 June. Meals will be served during the course as follows: breakfast at 08.00, lunch at 13.00 and dinner at 19.00. The course starts at 09.00 and finishes at 17.00 each day.

The course centre has full leisure facilities for your group to relax. Wednesday 22 June will be a half day, and during the afternoon there will be an organised programme of activities. In your group, nearly everyone enjoys swimming and tennis; some students enjoy sightseeing and shopping; others enjoy quiet indoor activities and games. The swimming pool is open only at the weekend, but the tennis courts are open every day. There is a free bus which can be pre-booked for visits away from the course centre. You will need the bus to transport everyone from and to the airport.

Three people in your group are vegans, and one girl is partially sighted and will need the course materials in large print.

As you are studying IGCSE South American Geography, it would be very helpful if the course organisers were aware of this in order to plan the most useful course sessions for you.

COURSE APPLICATION FORM

Name of your organisation: _____

Address: _____

Course required: _____

Total number of people: _____

Duration of stay:

From: _____   To: _____

Student accommodation:

Male rooms: _____   Female rooms: _____

Activities for group (please tick):

☐ Swimming   ☐ Basketball   ☐ Sightseeing   ☐ Indoor games

Suggestions for other activities:

```



```

Meal times:

Please delete times NOT required

Breakfast   07.00   08.00
Lunch   12.00   13.00
Dinner   19.00   20.00

Special requests:

a _____

b _____

c _____

In the space below, write one sentence of between 12 and 20 words in which you say why your class wants to attend the Humanities course in Belize.

```



```

Read the following text about the recycling logo and complete the notes on page 64.

Möbius and the recycling logo

It is difficult to miss the triangle of three bent arrows that represents recycling. It appears in newspapers and magazines and on bottles, cans, envelopes, cardboard boxes and other containers.

But have you noticed that there are two versions of the recycling symbol? The difference between them lies in the direction of the twist in one of the three arrows that make up the symbol.

A Mathematics professor, Cliff Long, noticed that the arrows of the standard recycling symbol are twisted in such a way that if they were joined together in a continuous ribbon they would form a Möbius band. A Möbius band has only one side and one edge. You can make a Möbius band by gluing together the two ends of a long strip of paper after giving one end half a twist. This curious object is named after the astronomer and mathematician August Ferdinand Möbius (1790–1868), a professor at the University of Leipzig, who published his discovery about one-sided surfaces in 1865.

One day, Professor Long noticed a second version of the recycling symbol. This new version aroused his interest, and he carefuly compared it with the one that was already familiar to him. He discovered that the new symbol was based on a one-sided band formed by gluing together the two ends of a long strip of paper after giving one end three half twists instead of just one. This second symbol probably came about through human error, as the original recycling symbol was designed by a student, Gary Anderson, in a competition in 1970.

Because of the simplicity and clarity of Anderson's design, the recycling symbol has become widely used all over the world and is now as common as many international products. The symbol has been revised over the years, and there are now different versions to represent different aspects of recycling.

The version with the arrows within a circle means that the product contains a certain amount of recycled material:

white arrows + black circle = 100% recycled content in the product

black arrows + white circle = a percentage of recycled content in the product

outlined arrows + no circle = the product itself can be recycled

But the science behind the Möbius phenomenon has practical applications as well. Take a look at the belt that drives a car's radiator fan. Ordinarily, friction wears the belt out more quickly on the inside than the outside. But when the belt is made with a half twist, like the Möbius strip, it has only one side and wears out more evenly and slowly.

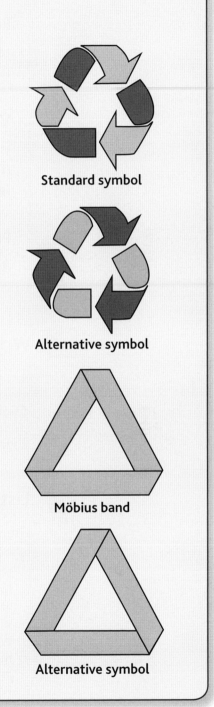

Standard symbol

Alternative symbol

Möbius band

Alternative symbol

Adapted from www.sciencenews.org, 21 November 2003, and www.mcmua.com, November 2003.

You are going to write a short article for your school magazine about the history of the recycling logo. Prepare some notes to use as the basis for your article.

Part 2

Important dates

1790–1868: **(a)** ......
1865: **(b)** ......
1970: **(c)** ......

Features of Möbius band

(d) ......
(e) ......

Versions of recycling symbol

White arrows + black circle
(f) ......
(g) ......

Practical application of Möbius band

(h) ......

 ## Writing: Exam Exercise 7

You recently attended a sports event at the new stadium in your home town. Write a letter to the manager of the stadium explaining why you were dissatisfied with the sports event and the new facilities, and asking for your money to be refunded. Your letter should be about 150–200 words long (Extended) or 100–150 words long (Core).

Track 4

Listening

Listen to an interview about a mathematical discovery and then answer the questions below. You will hear the interview twice.

a Why are prime numbers so important? [1]
b How many digits does the recently discovered prime number have? [1]
c Why might it be a waste of time to try to find a prime number? [1]
d What was the $50,000 prize awarded for? [1]
e How long did it take Michael Cameron's computer to find the prime? [1]
f What made Mr Cameron decide to start the search for a prime? [1]
g How many prime numbers are there? [1]
[Total: 7]

Unit 11:
Focus on reading skills

Exam Exercises 1 and 2

Vocabulary

1   Look at these sentences from Unit 11 in your Coursebook. What are the missing words? Each series of dots represents one word. Then add the missing figures to the gaps with dots in brackets (......).

   21.64   45   90   205   309.9

   a The largest .... has approximately (......) million subscribers.
   b The longest .... ever drawn measured (......) m.
   c The length of the longest ...... on a female is (......) cm.
   d A man in the USA stayed on a ...... for (......) days.
   e (......) million people died of ...... worldwide between 1918 and 1919.

2   There are ten events in the decathlon. Copy and complete the table, putting the events into the correct columns.

Throw	Jump	Run

Reading 1

3   Skim the four short texts on page **66** and decide which of the job titles below fits each one. What helps you to decide?

   forest firefighter   steeplejack   goldminer   deep-sea diver

A Numerous North Sea diving deaths in the 1970s and 1980s prompted a safety drive that slashed mortality rates. But divers still face perils as they work, sometimes in total darkness, hundreds of feet down in the oceans. Hazards of the job include the bends and jellyfish stings.

B The depths at which miners work – often more than two miles below the surface – mean that the effects of even minor earth tremors can be devastating, causing tunnels to collapse. In South Africa, where tremors are frequent, four men died and eleven others were trapped for days when hundreds of tons of rocks collapsed at the Orkney shaft, 100 miles south-west of Johannesburg, last year.

C The risk of accidental death is believed to be around one in 1,000 each year. In June last year, a man died after plunging 120 feet from the roof of Edinburgh Castle.

D In the United States, 136 pilots have lost their lives in the past 50 years as they attempted to douse flames with water. Smokejumpers, who parachute in, are even more vulnerable.

4 **a** Find two words in text **A** which have a similar meaning to 'dangers'.
  b What does *slashed* mean in text **A**: 'reduced' or 'increased'?
  c Which word in text **B** is similar in meaning to *vibrations*?
  d Give another word for *plunging* in text **C**.
  e Guess the meaning of *douse* in text **D**.

5 You are going to read a longer text on page **67**: 'It's the coldest, most isolated continent on earth. Why would anyone want to work there?' What do you think the text is about?

6 These words and phrases have been removed from the text. Use your dictionary to help you find out what they mean.
  a *auroral*
  b *motives*
  c *devoted*
  d *reigns*
  e *insomnia*
  f *swell*
  g *maintain*
  h *tang*

7 Here are the meanings of the words in Exercise **6**. Match each one with the correct word. Are your meanings from Exercise **6** the same?

   at the start of the day
   dedicated
   exists
   flavour
   increase
   look after
   reasons to do something
   sleeplessness

8 Read the text (page **67**) and complete the gaps with the words from Exercise **6**.

It's the coldest, most isolated continent on earth. Why would anyone want to work there?

Applications from steel erectors in response to an advert placed by the British Antarctic Survey to work in Antarctica are pouring in. The BAS is looking for workers to **(a)** ...... its southern-most research centre, the Halley base, during the continent's four-month summer.

Antarctica is the coldest and windiest continent on earth, and the Halley base is the remotest of the five British stations there. Each year, 15 staff see out the long winter, when temperatures fall as low as –55 °C and darkness **(b)** ...... for 105 days, relieved only by the spectacular **(c)** ...... displays.

Even in summer, when numbers on the base **(d)** ...... to 65, temperatures can plummet to –28 °C. Many staff develop chronic polar **(e)** ...... because of the 24-hour daylight.

Everybody longs for fresh fruit and vegetables, since food supplies arrive just twice a year and must be dragged 12 km from the coast. One former staff member recalls his colleagues fantasising endlessly about the **(f)** ...... of tomatoes.

And people need to be sure that they can get on with the rest of the team: the nearest neighbours are 30 km away and rather short on conversation, being emperor penguins.

The Halley site, on the Brunt Ice Shelf, has been occupied by the British since 1956, but the first four bases had to be abandoned because they were crushed by ice.

The steel erectors will have to save the current set of buildings by jacking up the steel legs supporting the steel platforms, to keep them clear of the snowfall. They will also put up new masts and other structures to assist with research.

The centre is best known for its work in monitoring the hole in the ozone layer, but it also studies atmospheric pollution, sea-level rise, climate change and geology.

But while scientists have often **(g)** ...... their lives to examining particular phenomena, support staff on the bases have other **(h)** .... Many find that a four-month contract is an ideal way to save money: pay begins at £15,000 a year; all accommodation, food and clothing come free; and there is nowhere to spend any money.

Adapted from an article by Tania Branigan in *The Guardian*, 6 August 2001.

9   Answer the following questions.

a   What is the weather like in Antarctica? Give **two** pieces of information.

b   What is the difference between the lowest summer and winter temperatures?

c   What happens to many people because of the 24-hour daylight in summer?

d   Why did the British have to leave the first four bases?

e   Apart from the ozone layer, what else do scientists at the Halley base study? Give **four** things.

f   List **four** points of advice you would give to someone applying for the job in Antarctica.

 Research

10   Look at the decathlon events in Exercise **2**. Use a bilingual dictionary to find out what they are in your own language.

11   Use a map or an atlas to identify the places mentioned in the text you have just read.

Writing 1

12 Write an application for the job advertised in Antarctica. In your application, say why you think you are suited for the position advertised, and what your particular skills and expertise are. You may also want to ask some questions. Your letter should be about 150–200 words long (Extended) or 100–150 words long (Core).

 # Reading 2

13 Read the information about Nigel Mansell, who won the Formula One World Championship in 1992, driving a Williams car. As you read, make a timeline of events in his career. Your teacher will help you to get started.

The fans' favourite: the career of Nigel Mansell

In 14 seasons in Formula One, Nigel Mansell took part in 185 grands prix, winning 31 times. He also claimed 32 pole positions and won the World Championship in 1992 while driving for Williams. That year, he recorded nine wins in 16 races, combined with 14 poles. He also drove for Lotus and Ferrari.

Prior to winning the World Championship, Mansell's career was dogged by near-misses and bad luck. In 1986, he suffered a high-speed tyre failure at Adelaide with the title in his pocket, and, the following year, he injured his back and was unable to take part in the Japanese Grand Prix, again with the drivers' title at his mercy. In 1991, he was the runner-up to Ayrton Senna after spinning in the gravel at Suzuka, losing a wheel after a pit-stop in Estoril and suffering an electrical failure on the final lap while leading the Canadian Grand Prix.

Mansell parted company with Williams after winning the World title and spent the following year (1993) winning the IndyCar title in America. Two years later, in 1995, he attempted a comeback, but had considerable problems squeezing his body into a McLaren car!

Adapted from *Sunday Times Sport*, 8 January 2006.

 # Writing 2

14 In this unit, and in the Coursebook, you have read and talked about various jobs: athlete, explorer, racing driver, firefighter, steeplejack, goldminer, deep-sea diver. Now choose **one** job and write about why you would like to do it. Think about what the advantages of the job are in terms of salary and hours of work, as well as job satisfaction. Write about 150–200 words for the Extended curriculum or 100–150 words for the Core curriculum.

Language

15 The verbs below have been taken from Unit 11 in the Coursebook. Make a list of other words which can be formed from these verbs. Use your dictionary to help you.

Example: *conquer* → *conquered, conqueror, conquest*

a	*determine*	**e**	*dissuade*
b	*achieve*	**f**	*explore*
c	*succeed*	**g**	*isolate*
d	*perish*	**h**	*climb*

16 Choose a suitable word from Exercise 15 to complete each of these sentences. It could be a verb or a word which has been formed from the verb.

Example: *The lands of the conquered empire experienced many years of civil wars.*

a The man who took over Maria's job, her ...... , is a person with a lot of experience.

b Ivy is a very attractive plant, particularly when it has ...... over exterior walls.

c Everyone in the class ...... high IGCSE grades this year.

d This is an ...... case and is very unusual, and I don't think there will be another like it.

e All ...... goods always have a sell-by date on their packet.

f Everyone should be ...... from smoking as it is so unhealthy.

g He was a famous ...... who died on one of his expeditions.

h She always gets what she wants; she is a very ...... person.

17 In the Coursebook, there are many examples of comparatives and superlatives. Copy and complete the table.

Adjective	Comparative	Superlative
tall	taller	tallest
thin		
cheap		
good		
bad		
unhappy		
untidy		
clever		
lonely		
far		
much		
shy		

Part 3

18 Use other superlatives to complete these world records.

Example: *The fastest time taken by a woman to win the World Championship triathlon is 1 hour and 50 minutes.*

a The women of the Padaung tribe have the ...... necks in the world.
b The ...... person in medical history weighed 635 kg.
c The ...... ear hair sprouting from the outer ear was 13.2 cm.
d The ...... insect eats 86,000 times its own birth weight.
e The ...... dive measured was 483 m by an emperor penguin.
f The ...... animal in Australia is the rabbit, which eats crops, destroys seedlings and damages the soil with its burrows.
g The ...... hotel in the world is in Japan and dates back to AD 717.

19 Look at this sentence from the text about Antarctica. There are three superlatives which provide a detailed description:

Antarctica is the coldest and windiest continent on earth, and the Halley base is the remotest of the five British stations there.

Write five sentences of your own which use a combination of superlatives to give a full description of somewhere, somebody or something.

 VOCABULARY BOX

cartoon
The Italian word *cartone*, meaning 'strong, heavy paper', forms the origin for the word *cartoon*. Artists made initial sketches and drawings on *cartone*, and over time this meaning extended to drawings in newspapers and magazines.

elephant
The elephant is one of the largest mammals on land. It gets its name from its tusks, which are made of ivory. The Greek word for 'ivory' is *elephas*.

hero
From the Latin *heros* and Greek *heros*, meaning 'demi-god', *hero* originally meant 'someone who protects or defends'. Its modern meaning of 'an important character in a play or story' dates back to 1697.

tyre
An Old English word from about 1300, meaning 'the iron rim of a carriage wheel'. The original spelling was *tyre*, but this changed to *tire* in the 17th and 18th centuries. However, the spelling changed back to *tyre* in the early 18th century, and this is the standard in British English. American English uses *tire*.

Unit 12:
Focus on reading and writing skills

Exam Exercises 4 and 5

 ## Vocabulary

1 Here are the definitions of some words taken from the David Beckham text in Unit **12** of your Coursebook. What were the words in the text?

> against
> first appearance
> have a contract with
> help by a team player
> in second place
> job
> work position

2 Find **ten** words from the 'Good twin, bad twin' text on page **91** of your Coursebook in the wordsearch.

M	I	N	D	I	V	I	D	U	A	L
H	U	W	Z	N	Z	X	M	S	O	F
Q	H	L	W	X	M	C	N	L	P	W
M	P	W	T	G	B	I	K	P	P	C
M	Y	A	L	I	W	Q	O	C	O	N
K	Z	T	R	T	P	L	B	V	S	N
Q	M	K	H	E	A	L	T	J	I	P
F	C	Z	Q	R	N	H	E	R	T	A
T	R	I	P	L	E	T	S	S	E	I
P	C	G	G	F	P	Y	S	L	S	R
P	E	R	S	O	N	A	L	I	T	Y

3 Use **eight** of the words from the wordsearch to complete the following sentences from the text.

• My first encounter with the (a) ...... that (b) ...... come packaged as a (c) ...... came more than 20 years ago in my local supermarket.
• Ancient myths and modern movies are full of situations where twins are made to represent (d) ...... (e) ....
• (f) ...... have the job of ensuring that their (g) ...... have a chance to fulfil themselves, and to grow up to develop their (h) ...... potentials.

Reading 1

4   In the text below, 'Babbling babies have natural rhythm', find words which match the following definitions.

    a a quality that you have when you are born (adjective, paragraph **1**)
    b ideas or methods never used before (adjective, **1**)
    c completely (adverb, **2**)
    d clearly different from something else (adjective, **3**)
    e without having a clear pattern (adjective, **4**)

5   Read the text more closely and then complete the following sentences. Use your own words as far as possible. You will need to write short phrases, not single words.

    a Babbling used to be considered ...... but research now shows ....
    b In the research, scientists examined ...... and observed two things: ...... and ....
    c The scientists say that hearing babies with signing deaf parents make a type of rhythmic movement ...... which is ....
    d The babbling of children with deaf parents was ....
    e Nursery rhymes and the way people speak to babies ....

Babbling babies have natural rhythm

(1) Babies are born with an innate sense of rhythm that is essential for learning a language, according to a pioneering study of children who learnt 'silent babbling' using sign language. Babbling is common to all babies and was once thought to be merely the result of children learning to move their jaws. But research on the children of deaf parents indicates that a baby babbles to develop its inborn rhythm, which is critical for learning a language. The findings could help children with speech difficulties by providing a better understanding of how infants normally use patterns in the brain's language centres.

(2) Scientists studied babies with normal hearing of profoundly deaf parents and found that, in addition to the random hand movements made by all babies, the infants demonstrated 'silent babbling' using rudimentary signs. By fixing lights to the tips of babies' fingers and analysing their motion, researchers identified non-random movements within normal movements.

(3) The scientists, led by Professor Laura Ann Petitto, of Dartmouth College, New Hampshire, and McGill University, Montreal, write in *Nature*: 'Hearing babies with signing deaf parents make a special kind of movement with their hands, with a specific rhythmic pattern that is distinct from the other hand movements. We figured out that this kind of rhythmic movement was linguistic ... it was babbling, but with their hands.'

(4) The scientists compared three babies with normal hearing whose parents were profoundly deaf – and who therefore had little exposure to speech – with three babies born to hearing couples who talked to their children. The 'silent babbling' seen in the children of deaf parents was a lower, more rhythmic activity performed closer to the body than the ordinary, random hand movements of infants. Professor Petitto said: 'This dramatic distinction between the two types of hand movements indicates that babies ... can make use of the rhythmic patterns underlying human language.' The singsong way many people speak to babies and the patterns of speech in nursery rhymes could be used more effectively in helping handicapped children to speak earlier, the scientists said.

Adapted from an article by Steve Connor in *The Independent*, 6 September 2001.

Research

6 Use the Internet to find out as much as you can about the topic of the text you have read.

7 There are a number of unusual and difficult words in the text, apart from the ones you looked at in Exercise **4**. Choose **five** more and find out what they mean.

 # Writing 1

8 Use the notes you made in Exercise **5** to help you to answer the following question:

Read the article about babies and their ability to use a type of sign language with their hands. Write a summary of the results of the research carried out by scientists. You should write about 100 words. Write in your own words as far as possible.

 # Reading 2

9 You are going to read a magazine article on page **74** about the island of Bahrain, which is situated in the Arabian Gulf. Before you read, find Bahrain on a map or in an atlas. Which other countries are nearby? What do you know about them?

10 Read the following statements and decide whether they are true or false. You will be able to check them later.

   a By 2100, a tenth of Bahrain could be under water.
   b Rising sea levels are made worse by human activity.
   c It is now believed that sea levels are rising faster than previously thought.
   d Although only tiny, Bahrain is the world's third-worst polluter on a per capita basis.
   e Bahrain accounts for less than 0.1 per cent of total global CO_2 emissions.
   f As yet there is no firm legislation that forces countries to lower their CO_2 production.
   g The energy industry accounts for about 75 per cent of Bahrain's total emissions.

11 Look at these words and phrases taken from the text. What do they mean? Use a dictionary to help you.

   dumping   melt   fed into   ascertain   creates   ratified
   partake   legislation   initiative   saplings

12 Read the article on page **74** and check your answers to Exercise **10**. Also, check whether the meanings you thought of in Exercise **11** are correct.

13 Look at the text again and answer these questions.

   a Why is Bahrain at serious risk of flooding?
   b What would cause 22 per cent of Bahrain to disappear under water?
   c How is more water being fed into the world's oceans?
   d How much CO_2 does Bahrain produce every year?
   e What has Bahrain done to show its concern about sea-level rise? Give **three** examples from the text.

An inconvenient height above sea level

By 2100, a tenth of Bahrain could be under water. Rising global sea levels mean that low-lying islands like Bahrain are at serious risk of flooding. Recent studies have shown that, if the sea level were to rise by only two metres, 22 per cent of Bahrain would disappear beneath the Arabian Gulf. Indeed, areas such as Muharraq and Seef would look similar to Venice if such a rise were to occur.

What is sea-level rise?

Put simply, rising sea levels are made worse by human activity. We are dumping more and more carbon dioxide (CO_2) into the atmosphere, which is causing global temperatures to rise. These rising temperatures are causing the ice shelves to melt, which means that more water is being fed into the world's oceans. Naturally, this causes sea levels to rise. Although it is very difficult to ascertain exactly how much the sea level is expected to rise, it is now believed that sea levels are rising faster than previously thought.

Where does Bahrain come into this?

Although only tiny, Bahrain is the world's third-worst polluter on a per capita basis. In other words, the average Bahraini releases about 30.6 metric tonnes of CO_2 into the atmosphere every year. Numbers one and four on the list are Qatar and UAE respectively. However, if we put things into perspective, Bahrain accounts for less than 0.1 per cent of total global CO_2 emissions.

What is Bahrain doing to prevent this?

Bahrain is certainly aware of the potential dangers of sea-level rise, and several reports have been commissioned in order to understand the effects of climate change. These reports have emphasised the need to raise public awareness in order to bring about effective measures. In addition, Bahrain has taken a number of steps to illustrate its concern with sea-level rise.

Bahrain has ratified the Kyoto protocol, which calls for countries to reduce their CO_2 emissions, although, as a developing country, it is not actually obliged to partake. As yet, there is no firm legislation that forces countries to lower their CO_2 production. This is particularly relevant to the energy industry, which accounts for about 75 per cent of Bahrain's total emissions. However, events and projects aimed at raising public awareness are happening in the Kingdom. A recent royal initiative encouraged the planting of 9,000 saplings in order to help lower CO_2 levels. Some evidence of renewable energy can be seen in Bahrain's World Trade Centre. Three wind turbines have been incorporated into the building to provide up to 15 per cent of its energy needs.

Adapted from 'An Inconvenient Height Above Sea Level' by Marc Owen Jones, *Bahrain & Beyond*, Oct/Nov 2007, published by Magnum-Bigg LLC.

 Writing 2

14 You are going to give a talk about sea-level rise and how it will affect the island of Bahrain. Copy and complete the notes on page **75**.

What is sea-level rise?

- humans putting more CO_2 into atmosphere
- as a result ......
- and so ...... , which means more water in oceans and ......

Where does Bahrain come into this?

- world's ......
- annual CO_2 output per person = ...

What is Bahrain doing to prevent this?

- Kyoto protocol ratified, although ......
- trying to raise ......
- three wind turbines at World Trade Centre ......

 ## Language

15 Look at these phrases taken from the text about Vanessa Mae on page **88** of your Coursebook:

> … *as a* <u>bonus</u>*, a video* <u>montage</u> *set to …*
> … *now also lists singing in her* <u>repertoire</u>*,* <u>having</u> *added …*

The underlined words have been 'borrowed' from the French language. Many words which are commonly used in English have come from other languages.

Find the 'borrowed' word in each of the following sentences. Then guess which language English has borrowed it from (choose from the languages below).

French German Hindi Inuit (Eskimo)

- **a** A chameleon safely camouflages itself by adapting its skin to the background.
- **b** The husky dog is well suited to an extremely cold environment.
- **c** Quartz watches are normally very expensive but of excellent quality.
- **d** Children often go to a kindergarten before they start school.
- **e** The thugs were soon picked up by the police.
- **f** The bride's sari was made from gorgeous silk.
- **g** Even today, the waltz is one of the most popular ballroom dances.
- **h** The chauffeur brought the car round to the front of the hotel.
- **i** The soldier planned to work his way up the ranks from lieutenant.
- **j** They agreed that the best place to rendezvous would be the park.
- **k** We normally buy some pretzels and have them for breakfast.
- **l** An igloo does not look like a very cosy place to live.

16 Guess the meaning of the words from Exercise 15 according to their context in the sentences. Then look up the dictionary definition.

Word	Guessed meaning	Dictionary definition
montage	scene	an art form with parts pieced together to form one
repertoire	list of activities	all the plays, pieces of music, etc., which a performer performs

17 Look at these other 'borrowed' words. What do they mean? Use your dictionary to help you. Use each word in a sentence of your own.

a tycoon
b chimpanzee
c sleazy
d sable
e cocoa
f cosmonaut

 VOCABULARY BOX

khaki
This word comes from the Urdu for 'dusty'. The colour was first used on British army uniforms in India in 1846. Olive green was later added during World War I, to be used against muddy ground and trees and plants.

legislation
This word comes from the Latin *legis*, meaning 'law', and *lator*, meaning 'someone who proposes'. *Legislation* was first used in 1655.

rhythm
First used in English in about 1557, the word *rhythm* comes from the Latin *rhythmus*, meaning 'movement in time', and Greek *rhythmos*, meaning 'flow of movement'.

temperature
The Latin word *temperatura* had a similar meaning to 'moderate character'. The connection with heat and cold was first made in 1670 by both Boyle and Galileo. Its meaning of 'fever' dates from 1898.

Unit 13:
Focus on writing skills

Exam Exercises 6 and 7

 ## Vocabulary

1   Look quickly at the advertisement you studied on page **95** of your
    Coursebook – then close your book! How much can you remember? Fill
    the gaps with the words given:

> donate   fun   illegal   impact   impact   lifetime
> memories   peers   skip   volunteer

Bigs and Littles have **(a)** ...... together – and create **(b)** ...... that last a
(c) .... We call it 'Little moments ... Big magic'. Research on our
(d) ...... programmes points to the powerful, positive, lasting **(e)** ......
Bigs have on children's lives. Littles are:

- 52 per cent less likely to **(f)** ...... school
- 46 per cent less likely to begin using **(g)** ...... drugs
- more likely to get along with their families and **(h)** ....

Learn more about our proven **(i)** ......
Learn more about volunteering
Learn about our volunteer programmes
(j) ...... to Big Brothers Big Sisters

---

2   Use your dictionary to find a synonym or similar phrase for each of the
    words in Exercise 1.

 ## Reading 1

3   You are going to read a short text about henna, a plant which grows in
    Oman. Before you read, check the meaning of these words taken from the
    text. Use your dictionary to help you.

> *dye   fragrant   ground* (verb)   *ornamental   revive   soaking*

4   Quickly read the text and complete each gap with a word from Exercise **3**.

Hues of henna

Henna is a special plant with delicate, **(a)** ...... white to pale-yellow flowers that are used as a base for many perfumes. For hundreds and hundreds of years, its leaves have been carefully gathered and dried to obtain a reddish-brown **(b)** ...... for colouring the hair and decorating the skin.

Henna is described as a 'plant of paradise' that is highly respected and must not be cut down. The leaves contain powers to **(c)** ...... and refresh the senses, and have been used over time as both a medicine and a cosmetic. Its medicinal powers have treated headaches, burns, bee stings, smallpox and toothache, to name just a few. Fresh henna leaves are often chewed to freshen up the mouth or to cure bad breath.

Some women use henna to revive and cleanse tired feet and to remove dry skin. The leaves are collected and dried, then **(d)** ...... into a very fine powder that is mixed with lemon juice. The juice is extracted by **(e)** ...... broken-up dry lemons for about a day. This brownish juice is mixed with the henna powder until it becomes a very soft paste. Then, the paste is covered and left to stand for about a day before it is used.

Henna is also famous globally as a hair colourant. Sometimes, henna powder is mixed with red tea to give a light red hair dye. To achieve a warm, dark colour, the henna is simply mixed with water. If water and yoghurt are mixed with the powder, an effective hair conditioner is produced, but only if the henna is left on the hair for at least three hours!

Henna is an ancient and very special plant that remains a strong traditional, medicinal and cosmetic product. Today, this historical 'plant of paradise' is best known for its **(f)** ...... applications to the body that have become fashionable all over the world.

Adapted from 'Hues of Henna' by Sarah White-Bait Al Zuhair, *Wings of Oman*, 2006..

 ## Research

5   Find out more about henna. Use the Internet or any other source of information available to you. Prepare the information you find and produce a leaflet or small poster to present to your class.

 ## Writing 1

6   Read the exam-practice question on page 79, and the sample answers written by two students.

Write an article for your school or college magazine about what you think is the most important piece of equipment in your life today.

The pictures above may give you some ideas, but you are free to choose something different.

In your article, you should include the following:

- the name of the piece of equipment, and what it does
- what its benefit is to you
- your reasons for choosing it.

Your article should be about 150–200 words long (Extended) or 100–150 words long (Core).

Student A

I think spaceship is one of the most important pieces of equipment for me. It offeres very quick transporting to space. Before peoples used to travel by animals and planes but nowdays they don't. It benefits to me because it means that I can go to the moon and mars and see other planets a very long distance from here. I can get there in a very quick time – much more quickly than on a horse or a donkey. They are quite safe but sometimes there are accidents and people use to die. It costs a lot of money to go to the moon and I don't think I will be able ever to pay a ticket but I really want to go one day until I die.

(128 words)

Student B

Have you ever concidered what your life would be like without all those things which make it so comfortible and easy? Yes, I'm talking about your mobil phone, camcorder, microwave oven, CD walkman, PS2, DVD player, and even youre coffee frappe whisker!

If you could keep only one thing, wich one would it be? Well, for me, there's no question that I would have to keep my mobil phone becouse it's more than just a way to call people, isn't it? You can send messiges, use your phone as a diary, keep notes in it, and of course play games! Without my mobil, nowadays I would be completly lost.

Whatever did we do before we had mobils? Did we really use those public telephones whenever we wanted to make a call? I can hardly remember writting things in a diary, and the days of having nothing to do while waiting for a friend to turn up are gone forever now that mobils have such a great selection of games!

Without my mobil I would be lost with nothing to do.

(180 words)

Which is the better answer? Why? Copy the table and make a list of the weak and strong areas in each piece of writing.

Student A		Student B	
Weak	**Strong**	**Weak**	**Strong**
no paragraphs		spelling	

7   Look at the two pieces of writing again and answer these questions for each one.

  a Is the writing enjoyable to read?
  b Is there a clear beginning and ending?
  c Are there many mistakes in grammar, punctuation and spelling?
  d Have the points in the question been answered?
  e Has the student included their own ideas?

 ## Reading 2

8   You are going to read an information leaflet about the South African Young Voices Network (SAYVON). Before you read, why do you think such an organisation exists? What is its purpose and goals? Who belongs to this organisation?

9   There are five paragraphs for you to read. Look at them quickly and decide on a suitable heading for each one.

Youth and the right to participate: the South African Young Voices Network (SAYVON)

(a) ......
The South African Young Voices Network (SAYVON) is a membership-based network that consists of 30 youth organisations from Gauteng, Limpopo, Kwa-Zulu Natal and Western Cape. The network gives a forum to young people from different backgrounds to share ideas, exchange experiences and learn from each other in the struggle for a better life.

(b) ......
The Network grew out of a process which prepared children and youth to play a role in the Earth Summit in 1992. The idea was to encourage young people to present their concerns to politicians and participate in the process to raise awareness of the need for sustainable development. Six thousand school children took part in the process, which ended with a Children's Hearing in Norway in 1990. Forty other countries organised similar activities, which culminated in the Global Children's Hearing that took place at the Earth Summit in 1992 in Rio de Janeiro, Brazil.

(c) ......
Young people, both boys and girls, are considered resources and are able to participate in decision-making processes.

(Continues on page 81 ...)

> **(... continued)**
>
> **(d)** ......
> SAYVON is a membership-based network of active youth groups who have strengthened their ability and capacity to mobilise for democratic and socio-economic change.
>
> **(e)** ......
> The National Youth Commission Act, 1996, broadly defines and refers to young people as those between 14 and 35. The United Nations General Assembly has, for statistical purposes, defined youth as being between 15 and 24 years, and acknowledges that the meaning of the term varies from one society to another. Taking all this into account, the South African Young Voices Network focuses on youth aged between 16 and 26 years.

Adapted from www.npaid.org, 15 January 2008.

10 Here are the original five paragraph headings, but in the wrong order. Are any the same as or similar to yours? Match these headings with the five paragraphs above.

   Goal   History   Purpose   Target group   What is it?

11 Find **five** words or phrases in the text which you are unsure about. Use a dictionary to check the meanings.

 ## Writing 2

12 Look at your list of weak areas in the two pieces of writing in Exercise **6**. With a classmate, try to improve the two answers. Do not rewrite the complete composition.

13 Answer this **exam-type question:**

> You have just bought a new piece of equipment, such as a mobile phone, iPod or Wii. Write a letter to your English-speaking friend telling him/her about it.
>
> In your letter, you should explain:
> * what piece of equipment you have bought, and why
> * what it can do
> * how you think your life will be different with this piece of equipment.
>
> Your letter should be about 150–200 words long (Extended) or 100–150 words long (Core).

 ## Language

14 In the Scouting text on page **97** of your Coursebook, the infinitive clause is used as an object.

   Examples: *To continually build capital funds ...*

   To assist in funding ...

   To support research ...

This style is usually only used **formally**. **Informally**, we can use the *-ing* form:

Examples: *Continually building capital ...*

Supporting research ...

Assisting in funding ...

Rewrite these sentences using the informal *-ing* form.

a To meet often is a good solution.
b To eat late is not good for the digestion.
c To go to sleep early is a healthy option.
d To assist the old is beneficial to society.
e To save money is a good investment.

15 Write sentences of your own using these verbs in both the formal and informal forms.

a prepare
b campaign
c consume
d equip
e consider

16 In the Scouting text in the Coursebook, these descriptive words are used:

worthy   regional   worthwhile   environment-orientated

Which words could be used to describe the following organisations?

a World Health Organization
b United Nations
c Big Brothers Big Sisters
d Red Cross – Red Crescent
e SAYVON
f Worldwide Fund for Nature

17 These words have been taken from Unit **13**. Copy and complete the table. You might not be able to fill all the gaps.

Verb	Noun	Adjective
establish	establishment	established
		environmental
	activity	
direct		
	objective	
	campaign	
		participatory
train		
	consumer	
investigate		

18 Find words from the table in Exercise 17 which match these clues.

    a This word also means 'to eat'.
    b This word means the 'aim'.
    c A football coach (not the vehicle!) is also this.
    d A policeman would do this to the traffic.
    e A policeman would do this to a crime.
    f This word is made up of six syllables.
    g This word could also refer to a battle.
    h A live volcano normally has a lot of this.
    i This word is connected to ecology.

19 Look at the words in the **noun** column in Exercise 17 for 15 seconds (no more!). How many can you remember? Write them down. The first letter has been given to you.

    a e......   **e** o......   **i** c......
    b e......   **f** c......   **j** i......
    c a......   **g** p......
    d d......   **h** t......

 VOCABULARY BOX

democracy
This word comes from the Greek *demokratia*, which is made from *demos* ('common people') + *kratos* ('rule'). It was first used in English in about 1575.

henna
This word originates from the Arabic word *henna* for the small thorny tree whose leaves are used to make henna.

scout
This word originates indirectly from the Old French word *escouter*, meaning 'to listen', which comes in turn from the Latin *auscultare*, which is connected to the medical diagnostic procedure of listening to organs like the heart ('auscultation').

volcanoes
Volcanoes are named after Vulcan, the Roman god of fire. Volcanoes are categorised into three stages: **dormant**, which comes from the Latin *dormire*, meaning 'to sleep'; **active**, which comes from the Latin *activus* and means 'having physical movement'; and **extinct**, which is from the Latin *extinctus* and means 'no longer burning'.

volunteer
Originally, this word was used to mean someone who offers himself for military service, from the Latin *voluntarius*. The first use of the word *volunteer* in a non-military sense was in 1638.

Unit 14:
Focus on listening skills

Exam Questions 7 and 8

 Vocabulary

1 Match the verbs and nouns to make phrases from Unit 14 in your Coursebook. There are several possibilities.

Verbs	Nouns
provide	*care*
restore	*health*
alleviate	*people's health*
diagnose and treat	*illness*
prescribe and dispense	*common illnesses*
perform	*medicines*
promote	*suffering*
prevent	*minor surgery*

2 Complete the five gaps in the text using some of the phrases from Exercise 1. Then go to page 102 of your Coursebook and check your answers.

> Nurses care for the sick and injured in hospitals, where they work to restore health and **(a)** .... Many people are sent home from the hospital when they still need nursing care, so nurses often **(b)** ...... in the home that is very similar to the care they give to patients in the hospital. In clinics and health centres in communities which have few doctors, nurses **(c)** ...... , prescribe and dispense medications and even **(d)** .... Nurses are also increasingly working to **(e)** ...... and to prevent illness in all communities.

Adapted from www.wpro.who.int, 31 December 2007.

Reading

3 You are going to read a text on page 86 about Australia and listen to another text about the Caribbean. Both texts focus on animals. What do you know about Australia and the Caribbean? Make some notes on the following topics. Set your ideas out in a table. You might like to use an encyclopaedia or the Internet to help you.

a location
b language(s) spoken
c animals
d important towns
e country / continent / group of islands

Australia	Caribbean
a	a
b	b
c	c
d	d
e	e

4 Before you read, look at these words taken from the Australia text. What do they mean? Use your dictionary to help you.

a *bulky*   e *obstacles*
b *immature*   f *pouch*
c *mammal*   g *rear*
d *marsupial*   h *survive*

5 Complete the text (page 86) with the words from Exercise 4.

6 Answer these questions about the different paragraphs from the text.

a Which paragraph tells you what food kangaroos eat?
b Which paragraph tells you what *macropod* means?
c Which paragraph tells you about the kangaroo's sight and hearing?
d Which paragraph tells you how the kangaroo got its name?
e Which paragraph tells you where kangaroos live?
f Which paragraph tells you about young kangaroos?

7 Answer these questions.

a Why was the kangaroo chosen as a symbol of Australia?
b What are small species of kangaroo called?
c What size is a kangaroo when it is born?
d Where does a young kangaroo live during its first weeks?
e How does a kangaroo keep its balance?
f What do the unusually shaped legs and large tail of a kangaroo prevent it from doing?
g What does a kangaroo usually do during the day?

The symbol of Australia

(1) When European explorers first saw these strange hopping animals, they asked a native Australian aborigine what they were called. He replied 'kangaroo', which means 'I don't understand'. The explorers thought this was what the animal was called. And that's how the kangaroo got its name. The kangaroo was selected as a symbol of Australia to represent the country's progress because kangaroos are always moving forwards and never move backwards.

(2) A kangaroo is a **(a)** ...... **(b)** .... It is a macropod, which means 'big foot', and there are over 47 different species. The smaller ones are usually called wallabies. The largest is the Red Kangaroo, which stands taller than a man and can weigh anything up to 85 kilos. It is the largest marsupial in the world.

(3) Kangaroos usually have one baby annually. The young kangaroo, or joey, is born at a very **(c)** ...... stage, when it is only about 2 cm long and weighs less than a gram. Immediately after birth, it crawls up the mother's body and enters the **(d)** .... The baby attaches its mouth to one of four milk teats, which then enlarges to hold the young animal in place. After several weeks, the joey becomes more active and gradually spends more and more time outside the pouch, which it leaves completely between seven and ten months of age.

(4) Kangaroos move by hopping on their powerful **(e)** ...... legs. They use their long, thick tails to balance their bodies while hopping. A kangaroo can hop at speeds of up to 60 kmh and can leap over **(f)** ...... up to 3 m high. Because of the unusual shape of its legs and its **(g)** ...... tail, a kangaroo cannot walk or move backwards very easily. Kangaroos are found only in Australia, Tasmania and New Guinea.

(5) As grazing animals, kangaroos eat grass, young shoots and leaves of plants and trees. Kangaroos need very little water to **(h)** ...... and are capable of going for months without drinking at all. The kangaroo usually rests in the shade during the day and comes out to eat in the late afternoon and night, when it is much cooler.

(6) Kangaroos have good eyesight but only respond to moving objects. They have excellent hearing and can turn their large ears in all directions to pick up sounds. Kangaroos are social animals that live in groups or 'mobs' of up to 100 kangaroos.

Writing 1

8   Use your answers to the questions in Exercise 7 to write a summary of the information in the text. Do not write more than about 100 words.

Listening

Track 5

9   You are going to listen to a conservationist being interviewed about the world's smallest lizard, the Jaragua. Look at these questions and try to predict the answers before you listen to the interview.

  a   What is special about the Jaragua lizard?
  b   Where was the lizard discovered?
  c   Why is finding this particular lizard so important?
  d   Is it likely that a smaller lizard will be found in the near future?
  e   What other small animals live in the Caribbean?

f What problem faces the Caribbean's forest region?

g What have local people done to secure the future of the Caribbean's environment?

h What must the Jaragua lizard guard against?

10 Here are incomplete answers to the questions in Exercise **9**. Match them correctly to the questions.

A Because it's about as ...... as a land animal can be.
B Birds, frogs and ....
C ...... which may eat it.
D It's the world's ...... lizard.
E ....
F Only ...... remains and some species of animal may soon become ....
G The lizard was discovered in ...... different ....
H They have formed ...... organisations.

11 Listen to the interview and complete the answers to the questions in Exercise **10**.

 ## Writing 2

12 Write a short summary about the Jaragua lizard. Use the answers you wrote in Exercises **9** and **11**.

 ## Language

13 The words in the box are taken from the interview you listened to. Use them to complete a copy of the grid below. If you write the words in the correct space, the shaded area will reveal a word which means 'our surroundings'.

animal   bird   conservation   frog   insect   lizard
mammal   reptile   snake   species   tail

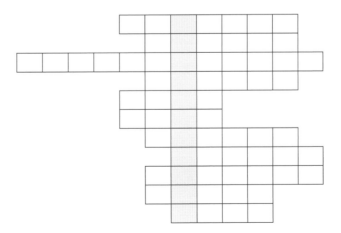

What is the word which means 'our surroundings'?

14 In Unit **14** of the Coursebook, *should* and *would* are used like this:

- ... *an appropriate memorial to her **should** be established.* (to show that something is desirable)
- *If you **would** like to receive ...* (to show an offer)

They can also be used like this:

- *would* – to talk about past habits
- *should/would* – a mixed form which can be used for requests, offers and sentences with 'if'
- *should* – to show obligation.

Identify the use of *should/would* in the following sentences.

a 'Would you like a cup of tea?'
b You **should** finish your homework now.
c As a child he **would** walk to school.
d If they read the newspapers they **would** understand more.

15 Write one sentence for each of the following:

a *should* for obligation
b *would* to talk about a past habit
c a sentence where *should* or *would* can be used equally
d *would* with 'if'
e *would* as an offer.

 VOCABULARY BOX

forest
The word *forest* comes from the Latin *forestem*. It was first used in 1297, meaning 'extensive tree-covered district', in particular districts used for royal hunting.

kangaroo
This comes from an Australian Aboriginal word *ganurru*, and was first used in 1770 by Captain Cook and the botanist Joseph Banks.

nurse
In the 12th century, the word *nurrice* meant 'foster-mother to a young child', from the Latin *nutricia* ('nurse, female teacher'). It was first used to mean 'someone who looks after the sick' towards the end of the 16th century.

reptile
A 14th-century word which originates from the Latin *repere*, which means 'to creep'.

Unit 15:
Exam practice

In this unit, you will have the opportunity to do some examination practice with exam-practice questions. These will focus on the examination areas covered in the previous four units: exam Exercises 1 and 2 (reading), 4 and 5 (reading and writing) and 6 and 7 (writing), and listening.

Reading: Exam Exercise 1

Read the leaflet below (which is aimed mainly at Western tourists) and then answer the questions which follow.

Weekend holiday breaks for all the family!

Middle East – Bahrain, Jordan, Kuwait, Lebanon, Oman, Qatar, Saudi Arabia, United Arab Emirates and Yemen

The mysteries of the East are waiting for you: from the ancient cities of Petra in Jordan to the oases in Saudi Arabia, there's always plenty to see and explore, and new experiences to be savoured.

For those seeking a holiday at any time of the year, the stunning beaches of Dubai in the United Arab Emirates are the place to be. Abu Dhabi is a modern city overflowing with wealth and vitality. Look for bargains in the gold market, and why not experience camel racing?

THINGS TO DO AND SEE
Jordan – Petra, spice route between Petra and Gaza
Oman – National Museum
Saudi Arabia – souks and markets
United Arab Emirates – gold market and souks, fine beaches, camel racing

Muscat is in the heart of Oman, a place to unwind and relax. Explore the fascinating castles, architectural sites, beaches and the old Muttrah souk, and discover more about Omani life in the city's National Museum.

HOTELS IN THE MIDDLE EAST

	Luxury*	Standard*
Jordan	$65	$37
Oman	$62	$38
Qatar	$75	$46
Saudi Arabia	$59	$42
UAE	$67	$47

*Prices are per person per night, based on two adults sharing a room, and including breakfast. Single occupancy is charged at double the price per person.

(Continues on page 90 ...)

(*... continued*)

Africa – Egypt, Eritrea, Gabon, Kenya, Morocco and Tunisia

The spice and variety of Africa are sure to appeal to everyone.

In Egypt, visit the land of the ancient pharaohs, follow the Nile from Cairo and be sure not to miss the Pyramids. Both the resorts of Sharm El Sheikh and Hurghada allow you to relax on the fine beaches. Try scuba diving and experience for yourself the beauty of the underwater world.

Morocco is full of Eastern promise. Go to the markets and bargain for jewellery, carpets and rugs, and a whole selection of beautiful items. Casablanca is a modern city with a traditional Moorish heart, where you won't want to miss the old palaces or peaceful gardens before enjoying the lively nightlife only Morocco can offer.

Kenya is for safaris. Look out for your favourite animals in their natural surroundings. Or shop for gifts in Nairobi.

Tunisia offers the chance for more sightseeing in the ancient walled town of Hammamet. Try the local cuisine or shop for a bargain.

Gabon offers plenty of local colour, with beautiful beaches and vast areas of rainforest full of wildlife. Nightlife is sophisticated with plenty to do, or visit the old quarter for a taste of local, traditional Africa.

HOTELS IN AFRICA

	Luxury*	Standard*
Egypt	$52	$25
Eritrea	$74	$41
Gabon	$60	$30
Kenya	$77	$48
Morocco	$72	$50

*Prices are per person per night, based on two adults sharing a room, and including breakfast. Single occupancy is charged at double the price per person, except in Kenya, where 50% is charged.

Call 00 800 22 333 444 and ask for 'Weekend Holiday Breaks' or visit our new website, www.weekendholidays.glo

a   Give **two** examples of mysteries of the East.   **[1]**
b   When is a good time to visit the beach in Dubai?   **[1]**
c   How can you find out more about life in Oman?   **[1]**
d   What is the cost of a standard room for one person in a Qatar hotel? **[1]**
e   In which country does the leaflet recommend trying scuba diving?   **[1]**
f   In which **two** countries can you see animals?   **[1]**
g   Where should you try local food?   **[1]**
h   How can you get more information?   **[1]**
                                                                                                             [Total: 8]

 ## Reading: Exam Exercise 2

Read the article on page **91** and then answer the questions which follow.

Gardening in the palm of your hand

The palm tree symbolises everything about tropical climates. It adds beauty to landscapes, lines our roads and grows in our gardens. Many palms are now placed outside front doors, on balconies and inside the home to give an exotic feel to living space.

Palm trees in hot climates are easy to grow and cultivate. You will need a seed, the right soil mix, a fertiliser and plenty of irrigation. There are dozens of books to help you get started, but for those of us who choose not to go this far, there is help close at hand in the form of ready-made palm trees to take home from your local garden centre.

The Green Desert garden centre spans more than 5,000 m² of land which contains an impressive collection of over 3,000 palm trees. The centre is owned and run by Ali Al Hamsa, who started the business nearly 20 years ago. He explained how to cultivate a palm tree from seed: 'You have to start before the spring. Place the palm seeds under 3 cm of special soil for them to germinate; in other words, so that they start to grow. This should be done early in the year, preferably in January or February, or early March, but it depends on the temperature. If you have enough water and good soil, the palm will grow very quickly.'

Palm trees vary greatly in size. You can buy small ones for the house, or grow them larger for planting in the garden. Some will grow as high as 20 metres. There are more than 3,000 species of palm tree around the world, with more being discovered all the time. However, most garden centres will only stock a small number of different types,

because of local climate conditions. The stock will also depend on local demand for different palms. The Green Desert offers three: a palm for the garden which produces dates; a second for the garden which does not have fruit; and the third is a smaller palm, which is ideal for growing inside the home or on a balcony.

The price varies enormously and is based entirely on the height of the palm tree. Some palms at the garden centre are small, only 30–40 cm in height, but nothing under one metre is ever sold. This is because smaller palms are not yet established.

'Once a palm reaches about 100 cm, it will be well established and will be able to survive the move from the garden centre to someone's home or garden,' says Ali Al Hamsa. 'A tree which is not established may suffer during transportation from the garden centre environment, which it is used to, to its new home, whether indoors or in the garden. People who buy palm trees – in fact, any plant from a garden centre – are often totally unaware of how a plant can suffer when it's moved. A common problem is that the plant is banged about in a car, causing the roots to loosen from the soil. This means that the plant can be starved of essential water. Another problem is that the leaves and branches may get knocked and broken, making the plant look damaged and ugly. Some plants may never recover from shocks like this!'

It is no surprise that palm trees have become increasingly popular in the home. Not only do they provide a tropical atmosphere – they have

also proved to be tolerant of a wide range of interior conditions, from air conditioning to central heating. They are practically maintenance-free. Surprisingly, an established indoor palm needs only a little sunlight for its leaves to retain their colour; also, it needs only a little water once a week to survive. If the roots of a palm drink a lot of water, the plant will grow, but this is not ideal when the palm is grown indoors. Palm trees in a pot in the home are watered to keep them alive, not to make them grow bigger.

If you are wondering how a palm tree might improve the look of your garden, you should go to an expert for advice and instructions on what to buy and how to plant it. But remember that palm trees are able to grow to great heights in a comparatively small area of land. However, because they have only one branch, palm trees are very easy to control, and there are no leaves to clear up. Unlike the leaves on most other trees, palm leaves do not fall, allowing us to enjoy the trees' subtle colours and textures, whatever the season.

Part 3

a   Where do palm trees provide an exotic feel to living space?
    Give **three** examples. [1]
b   What **three** items are required to grow a palm tree from seed? [1]
c   In what **two** ways can you get help if you want to grow a palm tree? [1]
d   What determines the month in which a palm seed should be planted? [1]

e Why do garden centres offer only a small selection of different
types of palm tree? **[2]**

f How is the price of a palm tree calculated? **[1]**

g Why are small palm trees not available to buy? **[1]**

h In which **two** ways can a plant suffer when it is damaged during
transport? **[2]**

i Why are palm trees becoming increasingly popular in the home?
Give **four** reasons. **[2]**

j What is the result of giving indoor palm trees too much water? **[1]**

k Give **one** advantage and **one** disadvantage of growing palm trees
in the garden. **[1]**

[Total: 14]

  ## Reading and writing: Exam Exercise 4

Read the article about Antarctica and then complete the task that follows.

The ice land of Antarctica

The evolution of Antarctica can be traced back as far as three billion years ago, to an age which most of us find difficult to conceive of. At that time, Antarctica did not exist as a separate continent but was connected to the southern continents which we now recognise as South America and Australia. A mere 150 million years ago, the separation of the continents began, and only 70 million years ago, Antarctica became isolated. This was the time when land mammals began to populate all the continents of the world.

Today, Antarctica is covered by polar ice, but fossils show that the climate and geography once supported a far wider and more abundant plant and animal life than the few seedless plants and insects which remain. About 200 million years ago, Antarctica was densely forested with trees and rainforest-type plants. During its next period of change, 80 to 100 million years ago, trees more suited to cooler temperatures began to flourish; as the continent continued its drift towards the South Pole, until about four million years ago, these trees slowly died out. Around one million years ago, Antarctica became glaciated, with the ice making the perfect environment for the fossilisation of reptiles, mammals and plants of all descriptions.

However, most of the continent's evolutionary record still lies buried deep beneath the ice, which makes up more than 95% of the surface area. Even experts have no idea what important treasures are concealed under the thick cover of ice, which in places is as much as 2,000 metres. As well as the ice, the difficult working conditions and the enormous expense of sending expeditions to the area have for many years restricted geological knowledge of Antarctica. More recently, great advances have been made by geologists in mapping the continent, and it is now known that the continent's geology is far more complex than previously thought.

There have been no significant earthquakes in the Antarctic region, making it the 'quietest' continent in terms of earthquake movement. However, in 1977, an unusually large earth movement did take place, with a magnitude of 6.4. The centre of the tremor was in the Bellingshausen Sea, to the west of Antarctica. This led geologists to believe that the region may in fact be more susceptible to earthquakes than had previously been thought.

You are going to give a talk to your school/college friends about the evolution of Antarctica. You have decided to use some information from the article in your talk. Make **two** short notes under each of these headings as a basis for your talk.

a   Three billion years ago   [2]
b   Between 150 million and 70 million years ago   [2]
c   Between four and one million years ago   [2]
d   1977–today   [2]

[Total: 8]

Reading and writing: Exam Exercise 5 (Core)

Imagine that you have given your talk to your school/college friends. Now your teacher wants you to follow this up with a written summary.

Look at your notes from the previous task. Using them to write a summary about the evolution of Antarctica.

Your summary should be one paragraph of not more than 70 words. You should use your own words as far as possible.

Reading and writing: Exam Exercise 5 (Extended)

Read the article about the game of chess. Write a summary explaining:

• the reasons why chess is not currently classified as a sport
• why people say that this situation should change.

Your summary should be about 100 words long, and you should use your own words as far as possible.

The 'sport' of chess

After many years of failed attempts by the British Chess Federation (BCF) to have the game of chess classified as a sport, it seems that the situation is soon to change. Once a game has been officially recognised as a sport, its governing bodies are entitled to apply to the government for funds which can be used to promote the sport and provide support for the people who play it. Experts argue that, because no public money is being invested in chess, there is a great deal of talent which is not being exploited.

Britain has always been one of the world's leading chess nations but, to continue to keep up with the best in the world, financial assistance is urgently needed. The equivalent of the BCF in Greece receives nearly half a million pounds from the Greek government each year.

The problem in classifying chess as a sport is that it does not meet all the necessary government criteria. Officially, chess is not 'physical' enough, but critics give the examples of snooker and motor racing, and point out that Formula One drivers even sit down to take part. The British government currently provides funds to a long list of sports, including arm wrestling, tug of war, skipping and sombo, a form of Russian wrestling; however, despite the fact that there are over three million chess players in the UK, the government has never provided any financial aid.

(*Continues on page 94 …*)

Part 3

> (*... continued*)
>
> As chess is one of the most mentally challenging games in the world, leading professional chess players have to undergo months of physically demanding training before major competitions, which often include games of up to seven hours' duration. The International Olympic Committee is considering chess for inclusion in future Olympic competitions.
>
> It costs about £6,000 per year to keep serious players involved in chess: lessons, travel to competitions, computer databases for analysis of rivals' tactics, books. These players say that, because chess requires so much physical and mental effort, it is ridiculous that it is still not recognised as a sport.

Writing: Exam Exercise 6

Your English-speaking pen friend is going to visit your country for the first time. S/he will be coming to stay with you and your family.

Write her/him a letter in which you:

- describe your local area
- explain some interesting activities that you could do together
- suggest some places worth visiting.

Begin your letter 'Dear ... '. (You do not need to write an address at the top.)

Your letter should be about 150–200 words long (Extended) or 100–150 words long (Core).

Writing: Exam Exercise 7

You are the secretary of an environmental group at your school. Write an article for your monthly newsletter encouraging other students to join the group.

Your article should include the following areas:

- why you are worried about the environment
- the environmental problems in your area
- what students can do to improve the environment.

Your letter should be about 150–200 words long (Extended) or 100–150 words long (Core).

Track 6

Listening

Listen to the talk about the future of DVDs and then answer the questions below. You will hear the talk twice.

a   What does the writer say was the advantage of using records? **[1]**
b   What have survived better than audio cassettes? **[1]**
c   When did compact discs first become available? **[1]**
d   Give **two** ways in which the storage capacity of a DVD can be increased. **[2]**
e   What are the **two** disadvantages of using DVDs? **[2]**

[Total: 7]

Unit 16:
Focus on reading skills

Exam Exercises 1 and 2

 ## Vocabulary

1   In Unit 16 (page 112) of your Coursebook, you matched words with definitions (Exercise 5). Find eight of the nine words in the wordsearch.

M	J	H	Z	C	F	T	D	D	N
I	J	X	N	L	J	T	E	M	Y
S	T	M	L	H	A	V	G	B	F
S	K	F	J	E	L	M	E	R	I
I	R	R	O	X	S	S	K	N	N
V	L	H	V	J	L	I	I	J	G
E	T	E	N	O	M	Q	C	K	I
S	J	M	P	Z	W	K	N	O	S
Q	R	P	J	A	R	G	O	N	N
F	Y	T	L	C	T	B	C	J	F

2   Match the words you found in the wordsearch with the definitions.

   a developed
   b messages or letters
   c careless, untidy
   d the words and phrases used in a language
   e to represent, or to be a sign of something
   f short, clear, with no unnecessary words
   g technical words or phrases
   h a possibility that something bad will happen

3   Look in your Coursebook to check your answers.

 ## Reading 1

4   You are going to read a newspaper article on page 96 about Berlin, in Germany. Before you read it, look at the notes (page 96) about the city of Berlin. Write something similar about where you live. You can add other points if you wish.

Berlin
complex public transport system
offers good night-time entertainment
rich in history
can eat out nearly any time of day
other points ...

5 Look at the words in the list below. Put each one into an appropriate category. Give each category a title. Use your dictionary to help you.

a *clubs*
b *cuisine*
c *eaterie*
d *entertainment*
e *fare*
f *Olympic Stadium*
g *Palace of Princesses*
h *Reichstag*
i *restaurants*
j *S-Bahn*
k *shopping*
l *tasty*
m *trams*
n *U-Bahn*

Public transport	?	?	?
fare			

6 Find the words from Exercise 5 in the text about Berlin.

7 Read the text below and answer the questions.

a List the methods of public transport which are available in Berlin.
b Apart from day tickets and seven-day tickets, which other type of public transport ticket can be used?
c When does food generally stop being available in Berlin's restaurants?
d Why was the Olympic Stadium originally built?
e Where was the seat of German government before Berlin?
f What is the latest time you can enter the Reichstag building?

Berlin: two in one

Berlin is one of the most interesting and exciting cities in the world. It is a true metropolis, with its own distinctive character and a vitality second to none. It has plenty to offer: culture, history, theatre and cinema, shopping, clubs, food, parks … the list is endless.

The public transport system in Berlin is exceptional, especially when you consider that two very different systems had to be combined after the Berlin Wall came down. The U-Bahn (underground train) has nine lines, and the S-Bahn (suburban railway) serves all parts of the city. Street trams still run in the former east part of Berlin. The city is divided into three zones for the purpose of using the public transport system, and most destinations can be reached with a single-fare ticket costing €2.10. Day tickets and seven-day tickets are also available.

Food in restaurants is generally available for up to twelve hours each day, starting from about midday. On every street corner, you will find an eaterie of some description. German food is not well known but it is gaining in popularity. A very popular place with business people is the Berlin Restaurant, which offers international cuisine as well as tasty local German dishes. The restaurant is beautifully decorated and, because of its high position, the views over the city are wonderful.

Although there is plenty to do during the day, Berlin really comes alive at night. The free magazines *Flyer* and *030*, available in bars and clubs all over Berlin, contain full details of everything that's happening. The busiest and most popular area of town is the Mitte, and Oranienburgerstrasse is the place to start your evening's entertainment.

Berlin is synonymous with culture and history: the Berlin Wall, the Brandenburg Gate, Castle Bellevue, Checkpoint Charlie, to name but a few of the highlights. The Olympic Stadium was commissioned by Adolf Hitler for the Olympic Games which were held in Berlin in 1936; the Reichstag is once again the seat of the German government after years of exile in Bonn. The building is open to the public until midnight, although the last entry is two hours earlier. Don't miss the Palace of Princesses, built in 1737 for the three daughters of Friedrich Wilhelm III, and the German Historical Museum, which dates back to 1695.

Writing 1

8   Imagine that you have visited Berlin on a short trip. Write a letter to a friend or family member telling them about your experiences. In your letter, remember to write about what you saw and what you did, and include any other important information. Your letter should be about 150–200 words long (Extended) or 100–150 words long (Core).

Reading 2

9   Earlier in this unit, you read a passage about Berlin, which has changed considerably during the last 300 years. How do you think schools in your country will change over the next 50 years? Copy the table on page **98** and make notes on schools past, present and future.

Part 4

	Past	Present	Future
size of classrooms	very large – about 60 students	about 30 students	
location of schools			
facilities provided			
students' attitudes			
uniforms			
subjects taught			
teachers			

10 Look at the title of the text on page **99**. What does *unveiled* refer to here?

- architectural plans have been shown
- people have been told about secret future plans
- students have given their ideas of how they want schools to be in the future

11 Match the words from the text (column **A**) to the correct meaning (column **B**). Use your dictionary to help you.

A	B
variable	built
dome	different
piloted	feelings
suburban	changed
constructed	six-sided
hexagonal	hemisphere
adjusted	out of the town centre
enhance	effect
morale	tested
impact	strengthen

'Schools of the future' unveiled

The government has unveiled eleven designs for the 'schools of the future', with features including variable-sized classrooms and huge glass domes. The project, to be piloted in 14 areas, follows a competition in which 50 architects took part. The schools, expected to open from 2006, were designed to fit their settings – urban, rural or suburban.

An estimated 180 schools will be constructed as part of the Building Schools for the Future scheme, which will be extended nationwide. In inner-city areas, some schools will have streets running underneath them, in an effort to save space. Indoor courtyards will provide open spaces, while, for less built-up areas, architects have designed outdoor classrooms. These will link with sports areas.

One design for crowded urban areas – 'the honeycomb' – has hexagonal classrooms, which can be 'shaped like pieces of honeycomb, so they can interlock, wrap and enclose'.

The new schools are expected to have a working life of between 30 and 60 years. The size of the classrooms will be adjusted according to the number in the group being taught. Single-storey schools in countryside areas and multi-storey schools in towns will try to achieve the same light and airy effect, using materials which enhance sunlight. It is believed that this will improve morale amongst the students, and so have a positive impact on educational standards. This is how the designs were chosen.

 ## Writing 2

12 Answer the questions about the text using the given words.

- **a** What two examples of classroom design are given?
  The two examples ...
- **b** How many schools are planned for the future?
  ... are planned.
- **c** Why will some schools have streets underneath them?
  Schools ...
- **d** What feature will schools in less built-up areas have?
  They will ...
- **e** What is special about the size of the classrooms?
  That ...
- **f** What is believed will help the students' morale?
  A ...
- **g** How is it thought the buildings will affect standards of education?
  It is ...
- **h** How long are the schools expected to be used for?
  They ...

Language

13 The text about Berlin on page **97** includes the following phrases:

- ... *destinations can be reached* ... (paragraph **2**)
- ... *you will find an eaterie* ... (**3**)

The words in blue are both examples of modal auxiliary verbs, which are used before the verb in the infinitive (without *to*). Other examples are *could, may, might, would, should* and *must*. As with all auxiliary verbs, modals in some way affect the meaning of the main verb.

Complete the sentences below using an appropriate modal. Some modals will need to be negative. Is there a choice of negative in any of the sentences?

a He's just been ill with a bad cold, so he ...... go swimming today.
b You ...... invite them, but don't you think there will be too many people?
c You really ...... get those presents sorted; it's nearly her birthday.
d He ...... fail this exam; otherwise he won't get his promotion.
e You ...... have got here on time if you had got the earlier bus.
f It ...... be worth checking how much bread we've got, in case we run out later.
g Do you think it's going to rain? ...... we take an umbrella?
h She ...... be at work now because she always goes home early on Tuesday.

14 Make sentences of your own using these modal verbs.

a	could	**e**	may
b	might	**f**	can't
c	shouldn't	**g**	won't
d	mustn't	**h**	couldn't

15 In the texts in Unit **16** of the Coursebook, the verbs *said, added* and *says* are used. Here are some other verbs you might see instead of *say* and *add*.

advised   answered   asked   demanded   joked
moaned   ordered   shouted   suggested

Make sentences of your own using these nine verbs. Use your dictionary to help you.

 VOCABULARY BOX

code
This word can be traced back to the Latin *codex*, which literally meant 'tree trunk'! From this we get the idea of something written on wood, and its modern-day meaning of a set of laws or rules.

display
From the Latin *displicare*, meaning 'to scatter' (*dis* = 'un-' or 'apart' + *plicare* = 'to fold'), *display* was used in relation to sails or flags on ships as early as 1292. Its more modern meaning has been in existence since about 1380.

public
This comes from the Latin word *poplicus*, meaning 'of the people'.

suburb
First used in around 1340, the word *suburb* means 'residential area outside a city or town'. It comes from the Latin word *suburbium*, which is made from *sub*, meaning 'near', and *urbs*, meaning 'city'.

Unit 17: Focus on reading and writing skills

Exam Exercises 4 and 5

  ## Thinking and vocabulary

1 How healthily do you eat? Write down everything that you ate yesterday.

Yesterday I ate ...
a cheese sandwich

2 Do this quiz to find out whether you do eat healthily. Use the list of things you ate yesterday to help you.

a How many portions of fruit did you eat yesterday?

b How many portions of bread, other cereals and potatoes did you eat yesterday?

c How many portions of crisps, cakes or chocolate did you eat yesterday?

d How many portions of meat, fish and pulses did you eat yesterday?

e How much water did you drink yesterday?

f How many portions of milk or dairy products did you eat yesterday?

3 Use the following information to check how healthily you eat. Statements a, b, c, and so on, match the categories a, b, c, and so on, in Exercise 2.

a You should eat at least five portions of fruit and vegetables every day. They contain vitamins and minerals that can help reduce the risk of heart disease and certain cancers.

b Anything from five to eleven portions in this category is fine. Increasing your consumption of these starchy foods will help to reduce the amount of fat and increase the amount of fibre in your diet.

Part 4

c Try to limit yourself to two portions a day. It's important to enjoy your food and these are special treats, so you shouldn't worry about eating them if you have a balanced diet.

d Two to three portions a day contribute to a balanced diet. These foods are excellent sources of protein, which is needed for growth and repair.

e You should drink about two litres of water every day. The human body is mostly water, so drinks are very important to keep our fluid intake correct.

f You should aim for two to three portions of dairy products a day. They are essential for the development of bones and teeth.

Reading 1

4 Look at these facts and figures.

> 60 per cent of all girls aged 14–15 say they want to lose weight.
> 25 per cent of boys aged 14–15 say they want to lose weight.

Answer these questions:

- Why do young people want to lose weight?
- What influences would make a young person unhappy with their body?
- What would you do if you thought your friend had eating problems?

5 Scan the 'Eating disorders' text on page **103** and find the required words.

Example: *Find a word in paragraph 1 that means 'illnesses'.* →
disorders

a Find a word in paragraph **1** that means 'important'.
b Find a phrase in paragraph **2** that means 'poor image of self'.
c Find a phrase in paragraph **2** that means 'demands from own age group'.
d Find a word in paragraph **2** that means 'reasons'.
e Find a word in paragraph **3** that means 'unwilling'.
f Find a word in paragraph **3** that means 'finding out what is wrong'.
g Find a phrase in paragraph **4** that means 'picture of oneself'.
h Find a word in paragraph **5** that means 'aware'.
i Find a word in paragraph **6** that means 'accept'.
j Find a word in paragraph **6** that means 'real'.

6 Look at the text and find evidence for the following statements.

Example: *Boys don't like to talk about themselves.*

Young males have traditionally been shy (paragraph 3)

a Doctors are learning to see when the problem is getting dangerous.
b Sufferers need to really want to improve.
c There is no real evidence of dieting illnesses.
d Boys are influenced by their friends.
e A boy's strong-looking body makes it difficult to see there is a problem.
f Numbers are going up.

7 Answer these questions based on the text.

  a Why is it difficult to give exact figures for eating disorders amongst teenagers?

  b What reason is given for why boys have eating disorders?

  c What don't boys like to talk about?

  d What haven't doctors been able to do up till now?

  e Why do boys now realise they can talk about their problem?

  f In what ways are gyms a problem?

  g What ways are suggested for dealing with the problem?

Eating disorders

(1) It is very hard to tell the exact figures because no government health department or agency has collected any statistics on eating disorders for either young males or young females. It has been shown that males are open to the same disease causes as young females, and that more males are suffering than ever before. It is being noted that there are small but significant increases.

(2) The main cause of these diseases is low self-esteem. Males face similar peer pressure with regard to body image and looks to that felt by young women. They are also teased and bullied for being overweight, have problems with girlfriends/boyfriends and have schoolwork stresses. These are all important factors.

(3) Young males have traditionally been too shy to talk about their problems. They are more reluctant to seek treatment and explain their feelings to parents and friends. Doctors have also had problems diagnosing the diseases in males. If a male has a well-muscled body and does a lot of exercise, then it is hard for a doctor to diagnose an eating disorder.

(4) But thanks to increased public information and awareness, boys are realising that they can finally talk about this issue. There has also been an increase in doctors' diagnoses. They are becoming much more aware of the warning signs. Another factor is the increase in the importance to young males of one of the disease causes – body image.

(5) Males are becoming more self-conscious about their looks. This cause of the disease in males is much more obvious than ever before. There has been a vast increase in the number of gyms trying to attract young males through their doors. Body-building has been proved to be a cause of eating disorders.

(6) It is important for sufferers to acknowledge and recognise that they have a problem. They also have to have a genuine desire to get better, as any treatment will require hard work and be a lengthy process.

Writing 1

8 Summarise the points in Exercise **3**.

  Example: a *Fruit can reduce the risk of certain illnesses.*

Reading 2

9 You are going to read a magazine article on page **104** about coconuts. Before you read, list as many things as you can about coconuts; for example, where they grow, what they are used for, what they look like, and so on.

Part 4

10 Look at the text and find and note down words or phrases which have similar meanings to the following.

a going on a journey by sea (paragraph 1)
b lack of enthusiasm (1)
c peace and quiet (1)
d attracting (1)
e green (2)
f attracts (2)
g look for shelter (3)
h are also used (5)
i rubbish (5)
j coconut shells (5)

Land of the coconuts

(1) When Columbus reached land after setting sail in 1492, he thought he had landed in the Indies when, in fact, he had reached an island in the Bahamas. Several years later, Vasco de Gama went one better by sailing around the Cape of Good Hope and landing at Calicut in the southern Indian state of Kerala. Over the centuries, Kerala's riches attracted the Greeks, Romans, Chinese and Britons. All have had something in common – a reluctance to leave. Today, nothing's changed, with promises of beaches and solitude luring visitors back time and again.

(2) Kerala is an incredibly verdant part of India. Over the years, naval merchants were attracted to its shores by the promises of spices, cotton and ivory. These days, it's the promise of leisurely holidays that entices foreigners to this southernmost state of India.

(3) Shaped like a banana leaf, the Kerala province is bordered by the Arabian Sea in the west and the Western Ghats mountains in the east. Wild tigers and elephants seek refuge in the wooded hills and the coastal beaches are clean and unspoilt. In between, hundreds of thousands of coconut palms make you wonder where you can stand without endangering your life! Keralites learn never to stand under the trees, to avoid falling coconuts and branches.

(4) The word *kerala* means 'land of the coconuts', and, when you arrive from Mumbai or Delhi, the wall-to-wall palm trees and whitewashed beaches seem as far away from the city and its traffic jams and fast lifestyle as you can imagine.

(5) Tourism is the major source of income, but fishing and coconut farming are also very important. Coconut juice makes a refreshing drink, and the white fruit can be eaten raw, used in sweets and for flavouring curries, or processed for its natural oil. As a coconut takes just 45 days to grow, one tree can produce several harvests a year, and every part of the plant has a use. The wood is used for making furniture, and the leaves for roofing. The leaf stems double as brooms for sweeping dust and debris from around the huts. After soaking in water for six months, the stringy husks are used for making ropes and twine.

(6) Kerala is made up of 14 districts, with Thiruvananthapuram the most southerly of them all. This is also Kerala's administrative capital; the financial capital is in Cochin, and the cultural capital in Thrissur. With just one million people out of a total regional population 30 times that number, Thiruvananthapuram is relatively small in a country which includes megacities such as Mumbai, Kolkata, Delhi and Chennai.

(7) Temperatures range between 26 and 36 Celsius, with high humidity levels of about 85 per cent. The main tourist season in Kerala is from November to March, when temperatures are pleasantly warm and humidity is reasonable. The monsoon season, when Kerala receives higher than normal rainfall and higher humidity, starts around the end of May and lasts until August.

Adapted from 'Kathakali and Coconuts' by Mark Daffey, *Open Skies*, March 2006.

 ## Research

11 Use a map or atlas to locate Kerala and other places and geographical features mentioned in the text above.

12 Draw your own map to include everything you found in Exercise 11. Illustrate your map in whatever way you want.

Writing 2

13 Use the 'Land of the coconuts' text on page 104 to complete the following notes.

> ## Location & geographical features
> - southernmost state of India
> - in the west bordered by **(a)** ......
> - Western Ghats **(b)** ......
> - **(c)** ......
>
> ## Economy
> - income from **(d)** ...... , **(e)** ...... and **(f)** ......
> - coconuts used for **(g)** ...... , **(h)** ...... and **(i)** ......
> - coconut grows in **(j)** ......
>
> ## Government & population
> - three capitals, for administration, finance and culture: **(k)** ...... , **(l)** ...... and **(m)** ......
> - region's total population = **(n)** ...... million

14 Read the text again, and your notes, then write a summary in which you include information about Kerala's location, climate and geographical features, its economy, and its population. You should use your own words as far as possible. Do not write more than about 100 words.

Language

15 Look at how the word *however* is used in the passage 'The North Pole' in Unit 17 of your Coursebook.

> *This year, however, he was able to take ...* (paragraph 2)
> *However, it is true ...* (paragraph 10)

- Both examples show how one idea contrasts with another. Other ways of expressing contrast are: *nevertheless, in spite of, on the other hand.*

Examples: *The company increased its profits this year. Nevertheless, salaries were not increased.*

In spite of the cold, they decided to go for a walk.

Complete these sentences with a suitable 'contrast' form.

a Temperatures are higher this year ....
b He studied very hard ....
c She worked very hard until late last night ....
d ...... they ran out of petrol.
e People on the island are extremely friendly ....

Part 4

f She speaks at least four languages ....

g His doctor told him to go on a strict diet ....

h The team played very well all year ....

16 Copy the table and complete the categories. Give yourself one minute to find as many words as you know.

Fruit	Dairy products	Liquids	Meat/fish	Cereals
bananas	cheese	cola		

17 Based on the information in this unit, write **six** pieces of advice to someone who wants to improve their diet. Use *should* in each of the sentences.

Example: *You should eat at least five pieces of fruit or vegetables every day.*

18 Look at the groups of words. Decide which word in each group does not belong, and state why.

Example: *butter milk eggs cheese.* → *Eggs are not a food produced from milk.*

a banana cherry melon apple

b beef veal chicken mutton

c polar bear penguin snow tiger elephant

d cow buffalo donkey cat

e India Pakistan Bangladesh China

f monsoon floods drought rain

19 Look at the words in Exercise **18**.

a Which word also means 'hen'?

b Which is a domestic animal?

c What do cows give us?

d Which country's capital city is Delhi?

e What can be eaten green and are known as 'plantains'?

f What is similar to a horse?

g Deserts always have these.

h Which bird cannot fly?

 VOCABULARY BOX

coconut
This word comes from the Spanish and Portuguese word *coco*, meaning 'smiling face' – think about the three holes at the base of the shell!

desert
This is a 12th-century word originally from the Latin *desertum*, which means 'abandoned place'. *Sahara*, as in the Sahara desert, comes from the Arabic *sahra*, and simply means 'desert'.

drink
Surprisingly, the origin of this word is not very clear, but it seems to come from the German *drincan*. Other European languages use words from a different root: Latin *biber*, Russian *pit*, Greek *bino*.

fruit
From the Latin word *fructus*, meaning 'fruit' or 'produce', the word *fruit* was first used in about 1175. At one time, it meant 'vegetable' as well.

Unit 18:
Focus on writing skills

Exam Exercises 6 and 7

 ## Thinking

1   Are there any single-sex schools (schools where there are either **only** boys or **only** girls at the school – not mixed) where you live? Give reasons why you would or would not like to go to a single-sex school.

Would like	Would not like

2   What do you think are the advantages and disadvantages of single-sex schools?

Advantages	Disadvantages

 ## Reading 1

3   Look at this statement taken from the text you are going to read. What do you think it means?

When girls go to a single-sex school, they stop being the audience and become the players.

4   You are now going to read the text on page **108**, 'Why a girls' school?' What information do you think the text will contain? Write down **three** ideas.

Example: *Teachers may expect more from girls.*

5   Skim the text (page **108**) and tick off any of your ideas from Exercise **4** that you find.

6 Find the following ideas in the text. State on which line each one can be found.

Example: *Girls tend to go on to higher education. (line 23)*

a Girls are more likely to apply for subjects that they would not traditionally choose.
b They perform better in examinations.
c As girls become older, they are less sure of their abilities.
d Teachers don't expect them to do as well.
e Girls have more chance to express themselves.
f Girls are more ambitious when they leave school.
g They don't have the same chances in mixed schools.
h There are fewer chances for them to get involved when it is a co-educational school.

Why a girls' school?

The school is the first all-girls' school in this area. The founding of the school was based on current research, which demonstrates that many girls attending co-educational (i.e. girls and boys together) schools do not receive equal opportunities to excel academically and socially. Girls' self-esteem and confidence in their abilities, particularly with regard to Maths and Science, fall during the middle-school years, narrowing their later choices of college courses and career paths.

It has been shown that girls in co-educational classrooms often have to struggle with:

– fewer opportunities to participate

– lowered teacher expectations

– limited encouragement in Maths and Science

– unequal sports opportunities

– insufficient female role models

– pressure to conform to stereotypes.

In contrast, at a girls' school, girls find out, not about equal opportunities, but about every opportunity. Girls experience the freedom to speak out, ask questions, debate issues and defend points of view. Girls fill every role at an all-girls' school: they are the speakers, thinkers, writers, singers, artists, scientists, athletes, actors and leaders. When girls go to a single-sex school, they stop being the audience and become the players.

We know that girls at single-sex schools do well academically. In general, school-leavers from all-girls' schools are more motivated, more accomplished and have higher ambitions than their peers from co-educational schools. They plan careers in Maths, Science and Technology four times more often than their peers from other schools. They score 30 per cent higher in tests than the girls' national average. In addition, almost 100 per cent of school-leavers from girls' schools go on to university and they are twice as likely to earn doctorates.

Writing 1

7 Look at this **exam-practice question**:

> Some people say that educating boys and girls separately produces much better results. Write an article for your school or college magazine in which you give your opinion about this. The comments below may give you some ideas, but you are free to use ideas of your own. Your article should be about 150–200 words long (Extended) or 100–150 words long (Core).
>
> 'Without boys and girls together, how can we discuss real issues?'
>
> **'I find that boys can be very disruptive in class, so I prefer not having them around.'**
>
> 'It's not natural to be separated in this way.'
>
> **'Having girls in the classroom with boys calms us down and makes us study harder.'**

Think back to the previous units which focused on writing. How will you approach this question? What stages do you need to go through? Discuss your strategy with a classmate and make a list.

8 Look at these two sample introductory paragraphs to the question above. Which do you think is the better introduction? Why?

Student A

I don't think that separating boys and girls at school is a good idea because we can both learn a lot from each other. Girls sometimes have a much better idea about things than we do and so if they are together with us in the classroom we can learn a lot of things from them.

Student B

The topic of whether to educate girls and boys together is a complex one, and I believe that there are many things to be considered. Personally, I am in favour of co-education, but I can understand the views of those who support single-sex education.

---

9 Write your own introductory paragraph to the question in Exercise 7. Before you start, think carefully about what information should go into the introduction.

10 Look at the two sample concluding paragraphs (on page 110) to the question above. Which do you think is the better conclusion? Why?

Student C

On balance, I think we need to continue to educate boys and girls separately. Despite the reservations outlined above, I believe that until we can guarantee the same or better results with boys and girls being educated together, we should not change the current situation.

Student D

It is my opinion that we should be in class together because we can learn from each other, we can have more fun, we can help each other, and so on.

11 Write your own concluding paragraph to the question. Before you start, think carefully about what information should go into the conclusion.

12 Answer this **exam-practice question**:

> Your headteacher has decided that all students in your school must take part in competitive team sports. Write an essay in which you give your opinion about compulsory competitive team sports in your school. The comments below may give you some ideas, but you are free to use ideas of your own. Your essay should be about 150–200 words long (Extended) or 100–150 words long (Core).
>
> 'Playing with your friends and against your friends can be confusing.'
>
> 'I like the chance to play together – we never do it otherwise.'
>
> 'This focus on competition and always having a winner is not healthy.'
>
> 'Who cares about winning and losing? Why can't we just have some fun?'

 Reading 2

13 The following five phrases have been removed from a text you are going to read about recycling. Skim the text (page 111) and decide which phrase fits in each gap.

Al Attar Street in downtown Cairo
As recycling has become the craze across the world,
But even Egypt
In so-called advanced countries,
Not so in the developing world.

14 Answer the following questions.

   a Give **four** examples of electrical products which are often thrown away.

   b What types of products do the repairmen in Cairo fix? Give **three** examples.

   c Why do Egyptians re-use so many products?

   d What is causing Cairo's repairmen to become anxious?

   e How do repairmen obtain the spare parts they need?

Recyling is a necessity – not a new craze

(a) ...... someone whose cell phone breaks down or becomes outdated usually tosses it away and gets a new, fancier model. Ditto for the VCR, DVD player, PS and even radios and watches, as well as cameras.

(b) ...... In Cairo, whole side streets and alleys are packed with electronics repairmen laboriously fixing circuits, keyboards and compact-disc lenses, charging around 25 Egyptian pounds (€3) for a standard repair.

(c) ...... Egyptians have continued to re-use almost everything, because recycling is a necessity, not a trend. Tiny repair shops are not unique to Cairo – they are a way of life for cities in African, Asian and other countries where people cannot afford to buy new electronic devices every time something fails.

(d) ...... is slowly transforming into a disposable-goods society as cheap electronics arrive from China, causing some Cairo repairmen to fear their generations-old shops, and the informal recycling industry they support, will not be around forever.

(e) ...... is probably the most famous repair area in this sprawling city of nearly 20 million people. Stereos blast Arabic pop music, and scooters swerve past the repairmen whose shops consist of a chair, tools and plenty of spare parts. Often, the repairmen buy an entire product, and then disassemble it for its components.

Adapted from 'In Cairo and much of the developing world, recyling is a necessity – not a new fad' by Anna Johnson for Associated Press Archive, 2007, reprinted with the permission of the Associated Press.

 ## Research

15 Find out what products can be recycled in your country. Does this vary from town to town or region to region? Is it easy to find somewhere to take things for recycling? What happens to the things you recycle? Where are they taken for recycling? How would you like the situation to improve?

 ## Writing 2

16 Imagine you have just spent a day in Cairo, during which you visited Al Attar street. Write a descriptive article for your school magazine in which you describe the street and what and who you saw there. Your article should be about 150–200 words long (Extended) or 100–150 words long (Core).

Language

17 Look at this sentence from the text 'Gum disease' in Unit **18** of your Coursebook (page **129**):

> *And anti-smoking groups would rather see people chewing than smoking.*

Would rather means 'prefer' and is followed by the verb in the infinitive without 'to'.

We often use the contracted form *'d rather.*

Example: *I'd rather stay, if you don't mind.*

We can also use *would rather* + object + past tense.

Example: *I'd rather you visited her later.*

Write sentences using the forms above for the following situations:

Example: *You don't want to stay late at a party.*

I'd rather we came home earlier.

a A friend wants you to lend him some money but you don't want to.
b You don't want to go for a walk as you want to watch TV.
c You don't want to eat the food that has been cooked for you.
d You want to go to the cinema and not to the theatre.
e You have to choose a day to visit a friend.
f You've been told to make a speech but you don't want to.

18 Look at the text 'A little pick-me-up for the consumer-boom's outcasts', on page **131** of your Coursebook, and find words which have the same meaning as those in column **A** below. Copy the table and complete column **B** with the equivalent word from the text. Do not worry about the other columns yet.

A	B	C	D
huge shop	*hypermarket*		
come out			
unusual			
doctor			
lucky			
lacking a job			
apartments			
cellar			
rules			
piled			
broken			
impossible			

19 Write the words you have found for column **B** in alphabetical order in column **C**.

20 Cover up columns **A**, **B** and **C**. How many of the words can you remember? Write them with the correct spelling in alphabetical order in column **D**. When you have finished, check to see whether all the words are correctly written.

 VOCABULARY BOX

cheap
Originally this word meant 'a purchase', from the Old English *ceap*. The word probably came from Latin *caupo*, meaning 'a tradesperson', and over the years the idea of 'at a small cost' developed.

girl
In about 1290, the word *gyrle* meant a child of either gender, but the origin of this word is unknown.

pavement
This is a 13th-century word which is originally from the Latin word *pavimentum*, meaning 'a beaten floor'.

This in turn comes from *pavire*, which means 'to beat' or 'to tread down'. American English uses the word *sidewalk*, which has a more literal meaning.

trend
In the late 16th century, this word meant 'running or bending in a certain direction' when used to describe a river, from the Old English word *trendan* ('to roll about or turn'). Its more modern meaning of 'fashion' is first recorded in 1863, but the adjective *trendy* was not used until 1962.

Unit 19:
Focus on listening skills

Listening exercises

  Thinking and vocabulary

1   Imagine you wish to work in the world of fashion. What different jobs do you think would be available in this area of work? Copy the table and list your ideas in the first column. Do not worry about the second column yet.

Example: *fashion buyer*	
a	
b	
c	
d	
e	

2   How does your list compare with the one below? In the second column, put a tick beside the jobs which also appear in the list below. Did you find any different ones?

   a fashion buyer
   b store manager
   c fashion photographer
   d costume designer
   e fashion designer
   f graphic designer
   g fashion journalist
   h public relations

3   Match the jobs in Exercise **2** with a description below or on page 115. The first one is done for you.

Whether in a studio or on location, you could be the person who takes the pictures.	c
You go to the show, chat with the designers, then write about it all for the magazines.	

If you think you can manage all the publicity and photo-calls of top models and designers, then this could be the job for you.	
Put your imagination and artistic talent to good use and you could be the person behind the look of magazines.	
Want to take control of which clothes appear in your favourite store? Going to the top fashion houses to buy the latest fashions could be the job for you.	
Want to style the stars? Think you can make your friends dress to impress?	
If you would love to manage a team and you have an interest in and love of fashion, this role could be perfect for you.	
Do you love theatre and musicals, and think you would enjoy researching, designing and making costumes for shows?	

4   Which job appeals to you most? Give **four** reasons why you would like to do it.

5   Which job appeals to you least? Give **four** reasons why you wouldn't like to do it.

Track 7

Listening

6   You are going to listen to an interview with a Marketing Assistant in the fashion world. Before you listen, decide if you think these statements are true or false.

- A lot of work experience will help you get a job.
- Making contacts is very important in the fashion industry.
- Having a university degree is not important.
- It's important to meet deadlines.
- People remember those who are confident.
- You should try to focus on one particular area of the fashion business.

7   You will hear the words/phrases in column **A** in the interview. What do they mean? Match them to the definitions in column **B**. Use your dictionary to help you.

A	B
PA	choices
relevant	connected
vital	personal assistant
deadline	changeable
invaluable	very important
fickle	time something must be completed by
options	up to date
on the pulse	necessary

Part 4

8 Look at these questions. Before you listen to the interview, identify the key word/s in each question.

a Where did the person being interviewed see the advert for her first job?
b What was the second job she applied for?
c What **two** things helped her get the second job?
d What **three** examples does she give of how going to university helped her?
e Why does she say work experience is important?
f What does she say you should always be on the lookout for?
g What shouldn't you do when you begin a job?
h Why does she say reading magazines will help in your job?

9 Listen to the interview and answer the questions in Exercise **8**.

10 How many of the statements from Exercise **6** did you guess correctly?

 Writing 1

11 Read the answers that Natasha Kafouros gave in her interview. What were the interviewer's questions?

Interviewer: Today, on *Fashion Plus*, we're very pleased to welcome Natasha Kafouros, winner of this year's Fashion Marketing award. Natasha, tell us something about how you got your current job.

Natasha Kafouros: Hello, Manuel. Well, I had always wanted to get into fashion and I applied for my first job when I saw a website advert. I was interviewed and got the job as PA to the Marketing Director in a large fashion company. Shortly after I started, a vacancy came up for the Marketing Assistant role in the same company, so I decided to try for it and got it!

Int'er: **(a)** ...... ?

N.K.: I had a lot of relevant work experience before I got this job, which helped me gain experience in the industry. Also, I was able to build up a large contacts list, which is really useful in the fashion business. I think that really helped me.

Int'er: **(b)** ...... ?

N.K.: It's very important to have a degree because it gives you lots of different skills that are vital in the working world.

Int'er: **(c)** ...... ?

N.K.: Well, communication skills, computer skills and, most importantly for my job, meeting deadlines!

Int'er: **(d)** ...... ?

N.K.: Firstly, get as much work experience as you can, in lots of different areas of the industry, so you can see which part you want to go into. Definitely create a contacts book and put absolutely everyone you meet in it – you never know when you might need them!

Int'er: That sounds like excellent advice. (e) ...... ?

N.K.: Always be on the lookout for jobs and opportunities. Spread the word that you are looking for something, and make yourself invaluable during work experience so that people will remember you! The fashion industry is not as fickle as you may think ...

Int'er: **(f)** ...... ?

N.K.: They know what they want and what they are looking for, so don't be scared to push your way in if you think you have what they want. The industry doesn't change easily. Don't be shy. It's much better to be confident, because this is another excellent way of making people remember you.

Int'er: Natasha, **(g)** ...... ?

N.K.: Be open to all the different areas of fashion; for example, public relations, styling, writing, marketing, buying, and so on. Try not to limit your options, especially at the beginning. And finally, read lots of fashion magazines, because this will help you to stay 'on the pulse' and remain in touch with all aspects of the business.

12 Read the transcript on pages 135–136 and check your answers.

Reading and vocabulary

13 Look at these words and phrases taken from the text you are going to read on page 118. Use your dictionary, and any other sources you like, to check you understand the meanings.

a *create an atmosphere*
b *sweeping the nation*
c *erase their individuality*
d *peer-pleasing designs*
e *ridicule*
f *mandatory*

14 Read the article about school uniforms (page 118). Then, using the information in the article, copy and complete the table.

Reasons for school uniforms	Reasons against school uniforms

Part 4

School uniforms

The introduction of school uniforms to state schools is not a new subject. Schools have a long history of using school uniforms to create an atmosphere of pride, loyalty and equality among the student population. There has always been an image of professionalism associated with having students wear a uniform. It provides for a more businesslike approach to learning, removing some of the distractions normally encountered when children feel they should possess the latest designer fashions, or follow the latest trend sweeping the nation at any given time.

School uniforms also tend to involve students more and make them part of a 'team' at the school. This is not so as to erase their individuality, but to include everyone on the same level as far as image and dress are concerned.

Another important factor in the use of school uniforms has been cost. With fashions constantly changing from year to year, and even from season to season, parents have always felt the pressure from their children to provide them with the latest peer-pleasing designs. Uniforms reduce the cost of keeping up, since they remain the same – day after day, year after year. And their cost, in relation to fashion merchandise, is very appealing over the long term.

Wearing a uniform at school, as opposed to wearing the latest fashions, may also help the child avoid ridicule, embarrassment or abuse from others that can be caused when the 'have-nots' are compared with the 'haves'. Uniforms assist in avoiding such conflicts by removing the chance for confrontation over clothing, at least during the child's time at school.

The debate will continue. But more and more people in education – students, parents, teachers and administrators – are convinced that mandatory school uniforms lead to success. They point out that pupils in private schools, who achieve impressive academic results, have traditionally worn uniforms. As a result, many state schools have also adopted a school-uniform policy – and the trend seems set to continue.

Adapted from www.communityonline.com, 16 January 2008.

 ## Research

15 Find out as much as you can about school uniforms in your country and in **four** other countries. Then, put all the information together in the form of a graph, chart or table, and be prepared to present your findings to your class.

 ## Writing 2

16 Using the information from the previous exercises, write a summary of the reasons why state schools are introducing school uniforms for their students. You should use your own words as far as possible. Do not write more than about 100 words.

Language

17 Look at how *whether ... or* is used in this sentence from earlier in the unit:

Whether in a studio or on location, you could be the person who takes the pictures.

Here is another example:

Whether you go in my car or in hers, you are going to be late.

Write five sentences using *whether ... or*.

18 What is the difference in meaning between the pairs of words below? Use your dictionary to help you.

Example: *newspaper / magazine* → *A newspaper usually comes out every day and normally covers all types of news; a magazine usually deals with specific areas and is normally weekly or monthly.*

  a retailing / buying
  b marketing / selling
  c styling / designing
  d career / job
  e picture / photograph
  f industry / factory
  g shy / nervous
  h confident / brave

19 Copy and complete the grid below, selecting words from Exercise **18**. You will find a word connected to this unit.

  a opposite in meaning to **g**
  b a job for a lifetime
  c could mean 'embarrassed'
  d picture taken with a camera
  e opposite of selling
  f place where things are produced
  g you might feel like this before an exam or job interview

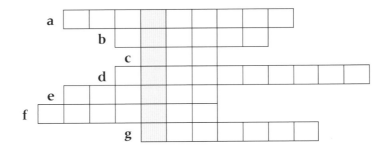

20 These words are related to the fashion industry. Use your dictionary to find out what they mean.

  a catwalk
  b chic
  c accessories
  d haute couture
  e designer wear
  f look
  g fashionistas

 VOCABULARY BOX

artist
Based on the Latin word *ars* ('art'), an *artist* was originally someone who 'cultivates the fine arts' – poetry, history, comedy, tragedy, music, dancing, astronomy. In the 17th century, the meaning expanded to mean anyone skilled in a craft or trade, but its modern meaning has in many ways reverted to the subject of art and design.

design
This word has many modern uses and originates from the Latin *designare* (*de-* = 'out' + *signare* = 'to mark or sign').

fashion
This is a 14th-century word which comes indirectly from the French *façon*, which means 'shape'. Its root is the Latin *facere*, which means 'to make'.

uniform
This word dates from 1540, meaning 'one form', from the Latin *uniformis* (*uni-* = 'one' + *forma* = 'form'). The noun meaning 'the clothes worn by a group' (as in *school uniform*) dates from the mid 18th century.

Unit 20:
Exam practice

This is a complete sample examination for you to practise your technique. Your teacher will tell you exactly what to do.

 ## Reading: Exam Exercise 1 (Extended)

Read the advertisement below about the Ecoworld Discovery Centre and then answer the questions which follow.

Ecoworld Discovery Centre

The future is here at Ecoworld Discovery Centre!

• Eco class for children!

Hands-on interactive games, challenging and fun! Discover the environmental world in an exciting and educational way. Special activities for different ages.

• Eco organic gardens!

Find out how to protect the environment in your own back garden! Learn practical and exciting tips to follow at home. Find out what lives under the grass and in the trees! Children under eight supervised by special helpers.

• Eco wind turbine!

Climb the 500 steps to the top of the 85-metre wind-turbine tower and see the amazing view of Carlstown and the river beyond. For a small extra charge, go on a special tour of the machine room (children under twelve not allowed without an adult).

• Eco gift shop and Eco restaurant!

Amazing gifts for all the family, each one specially chosen by our team of eco experts! The Eco restaurant has a great choice of snacks and drinks, with a wide range of vegetarian dishes available. There is access for wheelchair users to both the gift shop and the restaurant, and large-print food menus for sight-impaired visitors. Picnic area and free parking every day.

Kids – Special meals at reduced prices!

Opening times:
1 April–30 September: Monday–Friday 10 a.m.–6 p.m.; weekends: closes one hour later.
1 October–31 March: Monday–Friday closed; weekends: 10 a.m.–4 p.m.
Public holidays – closed.

School groups:
Weekdays 1 October–31 March: 10 a.m.–2 p.m. Booking essential.

Tel: 01882 733092

Fax: 01882 733093

a Where in the Ecoworld Discovery Centre can children of different ages do different activities? **[1]**

b Where can you learn about things which live and grow outdoors? **[1]**

c What can you see from the top of the tower? Give **two** things. **[1]**

d What do you have to do if you want to visit the machine room? **[1]**

e Give **three** ways in which Ecoworld hopes to encourage parents to bring their young children. **[2]**

f Give **three** pieces of information about the restaurant. **[1]**

g At what time does the centre close on Sundays in July? **[1]**

[Total: 8]

 ## Reading: Exam Exercise 2 (Extended)

Read the article below and then answer the questions which follow.

A day in the mountains

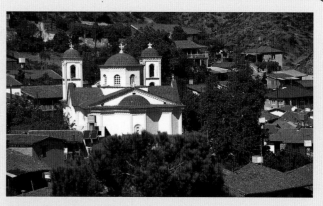

The Troodos area of Cyprus is only an hour's drive from the coast, so why not consider a day trip up into the mountains as a refreshing change from the beach? It will also be a wonderful opportunity to get away from the traffic and noise of the city and to breathe in some clean, pine-scented air while enjoying stunning views.

The Troodos mountains are the ideal location for hikers, bikers, nature lovers and skiers, as well as for those who simply want to picnic. If you want to ski, remember that the runs are not very long; however, the skiing facilities are excellent. Troodos is often said to be a good place to learn to ski because the slopes are not too demanding.

The impressive Troodos range of mountains, with its rugged scenery and vast pine and cedar forests, stretches across most of the western side of Cyprus. The summit of Mount Olympus stands at 1,950 m and offers panoramic views. Keen walkers and hikers will enjoy the nature trails laid out, which include carefully signposted information about the trees, flowers and shrubs encountered on the trail. The longest of these trails is the circular 12-km Atlantic Trail, which goes around Olympus at an altitude of about 1,700 to 1,750 m, with outstanding views of the whole island. There are over 120 endemic plants and flowers in the Troodos mountain range, including peonies, rock roses and orchids.

There are many important churches and monasteries in the mountains, including nine Byzantine painted churches, which are UNESCO World Heritage listed sites. The best-known monastery is the Monastery of Kykko, home to a very important icon, reputedly painted by Saint Luke. The tomb of Archbishop Makarios III, the first President of Cyprus, is nearby, looking towards the village of Panayia, where he was born.

The rustic charm of the mountain villages must be experienced and, if you go at the right time of the year, you will be able to buy cherries, plums, apples, grapes and pears, which are all at their freshest and best in the mountains. Each mountain village has its own special charm; perhaps you will try to fit in a number of these, and save others for your next visit. The village of Agros is famous for its aromatic rosewater, an important ingredient in the mouth-watering local cuisine. Kakopetria, at the head of the Solea valley, is well known for its excellent restaurants and beautifully renovated village houses. Lania is known as the village of the artists, while Platres is a hillside resort with a friendly atmosphere and numerous hotels and shops. Nearby are the perennial Caledonian Falls. Phoini, a village 4 km west of Platres, is famous for its pottery and trout farm.

If you are near the magnificent Cedar valley, you might also catch a glimpse of the Cyprus moufflon, the wild sheep which is endemic to Cyprus and whose male is characterised by large sickle-shaped horns. The moufflon is an inhabitant of the mountainous Paphos Forest, which covers 60,000 hectares in the west of the island. It is a protected species and, due to its tragic past, when it was hunted almost to extinction, some moufflon now live in protected enclosures. Here they can be admired without disturbing their peace.

a Why is it worth thinking about a day trip to the mountains? **[1]**

b Other than getting away from the noise and traffic in the town, what **two** benefits of the mountains are mentioned? **[2]**

c Who are the Troodos mountains ideal for? Give **four** examples. **[1]**

d Give **two** reasons why Troodos is a good place for beginners to ski. **[2]**

e Where in Cyprus are the mountains? **[1]**

f What information can mountain walkers find? **[1]**

g How high is the longest mountain trail? **[1]**

h What can be found in the mountains, other than plants and animals? **[1]**

i Why is the village of Panayia important? **[1]**

j What is sold in the mountain villages at certain times of the year? **[1]**

k In which **two** villages is good food guaranteed? **[1]**

l Why is the moufflon a protected species? **[1]**

[Total: 14]

Reading and writing: Exam Exercise 3 (Extended)

Read the following passage about Kadil Adallan and then complete the application form which follows.

Kadil Adallan is 16 years old and is currently attending the Capital School. The school's contact details are as follows:

telephone and fax: 246815
e-mail: capitalschool@arabianet.glo
website: www.capitalschool.ac.glo

Kadil lives at 46 Ruwi Street, Muscat, Oman. He does not have a telephone at home, but his mother's work telephone is 246993. Kadil checks his e-mails on a computer at school, and his e-mail address is kadilrunner@hotmail.glo.

Kadil is a very keen sprint athlete who has already represented his school in a number of events, including the 100- and 200-metre races. Two years ago, he won the Oman under-15s 200-metre race. He has also recently won an inter-school 100-metre race for students.

The municipality of Salalah (in the south of Oman, about 1,000 km from the capital, Muscat) is organising a sports day for students, and Kadil has decided to enter. The event takes place on 27 June. There is an entry fee of $28 for under-16s, and $45 for students 16 and over, which must be sent with the application form. Kadil thinks this is too expensive and he is hoping to find someone who will sponsor him. The organisers of the sports day want to attract as many sponsors as possible in order to raise money for children with special educational needs.

The closing date for applications is only three days away. Kadil has decided to ask his local sports club if they will pay his entry fee. His trainer at the club is Mrs Fatima Indiri; her address is 719 Salalah Road, Muscat, and her telephone number is 246114.

As Kadil does not live in Salalah, he will need transport to the sports day, and accommodation. There is a regular bus service between Muscat and Salalah, which costs $20 for a single ticket and $30 for a return. Students pay half price. The overnight journey takes twelve hours, departing from Muscat at six o'clock in the evening. The return bus from Salalah leaves at seven o'clock in the morning. Gulf Air operates flights between Muscat

(*Continues on page 124 ...*)

Part 4

(*... continued*)

and Salalah, and further information about times and prices is available from the event organisers. Kadil will get the bus on 25 June and return to Muscat on 28 June. The ticket money must be included with the application form.

Accommodation is available in the Salalah Hotel. A single room costs $75 per night, including breakfast. Kadil will need to pay for the hotel when he checks in. Lunch and dinner are provided by the organisers, and they have to be notified of any special dietary requirements. Kadil will need a room at the hotel for two nights, and he does not have any particular food requirements. Salalah municipality is offering a choice of entertainment on 27 and 28 June. Kadil would like to watch a film about famous athletes, or attend an exhibition about Omani culture.

Salalah sports day

Application Form

SECTION A – please complete in block capitals
Surname: _____   Initial: _____   Age: _____
Male/Female (please delete as appropriate)
Home address: _____
Telephone: _____   E-mail: _____

SECTION B
Running experience & competitions entered: _____
Name & address of proposed sponsor: _____
Telephone: _____   E-mail: _____

SECTION C
Arrival date and time: _____
Departure date and time: _____
Do you require transport?   YES   NO
Type of transport: bus   plane
Type of ticket (return/single): _____
Ticket price enclosed: $ _____
Entry fee enclosed: $28 $45
Do you require accommodation?   YES   NO
Number of nights: _____
Special food requirements (please list): _____
Entertainment (please tick first and second choices):

27 June ☐ basketball ☐ film night ☐ beach walk ☐ exhibition
28 June ☐ volleyball   ☐ exhibition   ☐ shopping   ☐ film night

SECTION D
Write one sentence of 12–20 words telling us why you think your application to join our sports day should be accepted.

_____
_____
_____
_____

Reading and writing: Exam Exercise 4 (Extended)

Read the following article about whaling and then answer the task which follows.

The history of whaling

Whales have been hunted for nearly 2,000 years, mainly for food but also as a source of fuel and material for making tools and weapons. The first whale hunters were Eskimos and American Indians but, in the 15th century, whales were also hunted in the seas off western Europe. Whalers from France and Spain ventured far from home in their pursuit of whales, some travelling as far as Iceland.

Later on, in the 17th century, Dutch and English fishermen built large fleets of whaling ships, having realised the enormous value of whale products. It is estimated that at times the Dutch had 300 ships at sea with more than 18,000 sailors on board. In the early 18th century, these fleets of ships were forced to hunt as far away as Greenland, as the number of whales closer to home decreased rapidly due to over-whaling. Towards the end of the 18th century, brick ovens were installed on whaling ships. These ovens allowed whalers to boil and process the precious whale blubber or fat at sea and store it in barrels, rather than stopping frequently at ports in order to offload supplies. This meant that whaling ships commonly stayed at sea for up to four years before returning home with their cargo.

During the 19th century, the Pacific and Arctic Oceans became the new hunting grounds. A fleet of more than 700 whaling ships from the USA dominated the world industry, which demanded more and more whale products up until the end of the century. With the rise of the petroleum industry, the need for whale blubber decreased rapidly, but the 20th century saw a dramatic rise in new uses for whale products.

The original Eskimo whalers sailed in skin boats and used harpoons to kill whales, which were attached to long ropes also made of skin. European and North American whalers used similar methods. Usually six men in a boat about 9 m long would go after a whale. The boat was equipped with harpoons and long ropes. A whaler would throw the harpoon and, once hit, the whale would swim away underwater, then resurface as it became exhausted, when it would be harpooned again. The whale was then strapped to the side of the boat, its fat would be removed, and the rest of the body would be thrown away.

In the mid 19th century, a gun was developed that fired harpoons which contained a small explosive charge. The gun could throw the harpoon much greater distances than a man, and this meant that faster-swimming whales could now be hunted.

Nowadays, helicopters, sonar and high-powered harpoon guns, as well as other technology, have made the whaling industry able to catch enormous quantities of whales. Whaling ships now have on-board equipment and laboratories for processing whales, which means that a whale as big as a prehistoric dinosaur can be completely processed in less than an hour.

You are going to give a talk to your school/college about the history of whaling.

You have decided to use some information from the article in your talk.

Make two short notes under each of these headings as a basis for your talk.

a 15th–17th centuries   [2]
b 18th century   [2]
c 19th century   [2]
d present day   [2]
                                                                  [Total: 8]

Part 4

Reading and writing: Exam Exercise 5 (Core)

Imagine that you have given your talk to your school/college friends. Now your teacher wants you to follow this up with a written summary.

Look at your notes from Exercise 4. Use them to write a summary about the history of whaling.

Your summary should be one paragraph of not more than 70 words. You should use your own words as far as possible.

  ## Reading and writing: Exam Exercise 5 (Extended)

Read the following article about cyclones. Write a summary in which you include information about:

- the wind speed of cyclones
- the location of cyclones.

Your summary should be about 100 words long, and you should use your own words as far as possible.

Extreme weather – the cyclone

Cyclones form as tropical depressions above warm seawater, and usually cover a huge area, often between 200 and 400 kilometres across. The majority of tropical depressions never actually reach the stage of becoming a cyclone, and simply lose their strength over a period of some days. Those that do become tropical cyclones may live for between a few hours and several weeks, but most last from five to ten days.

Wind speed

In the early stages of a tropical storm, the wind increases in strength from 'weak storm' status (65–87 kph) to gale-force status (up to 118 kph), which is typical of the speed of a tropical cyclone. The wind spirals towards a distinct centre, called the 'eye', which can be anything from 5 to 15 kilometres in diameter. As the wind speed of the spiral increases, atmospheric pressure drops rapidly, and the diameter of the eye may increase to as much as 200 kilometres. Many tropical storms will not actually develop any further than this, and while there may be occasional wind speeds in excess of 120 kph, the storms never actually become tropical cyclones.

Travel over land

Cyclones which travel over a land surface lose a considerable amount of their energy and wind speed due to the friction created with the land contours. In mountainous areas of Vietnam, most cyclones die out very quickly; however, in the flat plateau areas of Western Australia, there is little in the natural geography to create the friction necessary to reduce the strength of a cyclone. Cyclones in this area commonly travel more than 1,500 kilometres. In 1969 in the United States, hurricane Camille travelled 1,800 kilometres, and while it lost much of its strength, it kept its structure.

Location

Nowadays, every cyclonic disturbance is detected by satellite. The major areas in the North Atlantic are: south of the Cape Verde Islands, east of the Lesser Antilles, the western Caribbean Sea and the Gulf of Mexico. Water temperatures in the latter two areas rise quickly in the early summer months, causing cyclones to evolve before other areas. As water temperatures rise to 28 °C and more in late July and August, the number of cyclones across the Atlantic area increases. The storms travel west, gathering strength, and then curve back. By mid to late September, as water temperatures begin to cool, the area of cyclone origin returns to the Caribbean and the Gulf of Mexico.

Writing: Exam Exercise 6

COMPETITION

YOUNG SPORTS WRITER

We would like you to tell us about a sports event you have recently attended.

What was the sport? Where did it take place?

Why did you go? Why was it memorable?

Write us a short article.

Fantastic prizes to be won!

Best entries will be printed in the newspaper!

You have just read this announcement in a newspaper and have decided to enter the competition. Write your entry. Your article should be about 150–200 words long (Extended) or 100–150 words long (Core). Don't forget to include:

- where you went and what the sports event was
- why you went
- why you have chosen to write about it.

You will receive up to nine marks for the content of your article and up to nine marks for the style and accuracy of your language.

 # Writing: Exam Exercise 7

Here are some different views on using animals for medical research:

'It is wrong to harm or kill animals just to help people – animals have feelings too!'

'It is essential that we test new medicines on animals before using them on people. What else can we do?'

'I think we should only use animals for things which will not harm them, such as beauty products.'

'There is no excuse for testing lipstick and other make-up on animals. People do not need make-up! If we need to test new products, we should test them on ourselves.'

Write an article for your school magazine explaining what you think about using animals for medical research. The comments above may give you some ideas but you are free to use any ideas of your own. Your article should be about 150–200 words long (Extended) or 100–150 words long (Core). You will receive up to nine marks for the content of your article and up to nine marks for the style and accuracy of your language.

Part 4

Track 1

Unit 4: Listening, Exercise 10

Listen to this interview with a spokesperson from the Food Advertising Unit and complete the notes provided in your Workbook. You will hear the interview twice.

Interviewer: Hello, and welcome to our weekly radio programme on advertising. Today we have here in the studio Margarita Assudo, spokesperson for the Food Advertising Unit.

Margarita Assudo: Hello.

Int'er: Margarita, what do parents and adults think about advertising to children?

M.A.: Advertising to kids, and particularly food advertising to kids, is a subject of much controversy in the UK. Some parents believe that advertising manipulates their children into wanting things they don't need, whilst others believe that advertising helps them to choose things their children will like.

Int'er: I understand some research has been carried out to determine what parents think about this. What does the research tell us?

M.A.: Yes. According to a report on the Promotion of Food to Children, published in 2001, there is actually little public concern over food advertising. Children understand that television commercials are designed to make them want products and this understanding is clearly apparent, even amongst the seven- to nine-year-olds, the youngest children in the group discussions.

Int'er: I see. But do parents want stricter controls over advertising aimed at children?

M.A.: Surprisingly, no. Parents see no need for additional rules or laws regarding advertising. In a study in the year 2000, commissioned by the Advertising Education Forum, 86 per cent of parents did not mention TV advertising as one of the five major influences on their food choice. In the UK, only five per cent mentioned advertising as an influence; in Denmark it was 41 per cent. In Sweden, where TV advertising to children is banned, 11 per cent of parents felt it to be a major influence.

Int'er: So, in general then, do parents and adults see advertising to children as a major problem?

M.A.: Not really, no. Across several studies of parental attitudes, there is general agreement that advertising is not one of the major influences on their children and that, broadly, parents, brothers and sisters, friends and school are more powerful.

Int'er: Margarita, does advertising have any effect on diet-related problems?

Appendix

M.A.: Not really, no. For example, Norway and Belgium have three or four times fewer food advertisements per hour on average than Germany, Denmark, Finland and the Netherlands, yet suffer from higher levels of obesity. In Quebec, where advertising to children on TV has been banned for over 20 years, levels of obesity are no lower than in any other Canadian provinces.

Int'er: Is there any scientific evidence of the extent of advertising's influence on food choice?

M.A.: Most certainly, although it is difficult to come to any conclusions because the facts seem to contradict themselves.

Int'er: Can you give us an example?

M.A.: Well, in 2003 it was found that food advertising had an effect on children's preferences, buying behaviour and consumption. However, there is no reason to assume that advertising will negatively affect a child's dietary health. It can influence it, but this influence could just as easily be positive as negative.

Int'er: Yes, I can see that.

M.A.: Children today are exposed to a wider range of influences than any other generation. Restricting advertising during children's programming would not protect them from commercial messages. Understanding the role of marketing and developing the ability to make critical comparisons is an essential part of growing up and becoming a citizen in a free-market democracy.

Int'er: Margarita, thank you for a very interesting and useful discussion. Now let's go to our reporter in …

Track 2

Unit 5: Listening

Listen to this interview about dangers in the home and complete the notes provided in your Workbook. You will hear the interview twice.

Interviewer: Good afternoon, and welcome to *Good Home*. My guest today is Corina Montero, a college lecturer who specialises in children's safety in the home.

Corina Montero: Hello.

Int'er: Corina, I would have thought that the home was the safest place for children to be!

C.M.: Well, yes, it should be, but there are unexpected dangers which we all need to be aware of.

Int'er: Dangers? In the home?

C.M.: Yes! Although most things in the home are safe, it is nonetheless important to note that safety is perhaps the most important life skill that children need to learn from an early age.

Int'er: You're joking!

C.M.: Unfortunately, I'm not. Most accidents in the home happen in the living room, bedroom, on the stairs and in the kitchen. Falls account for the greatest number of accidents, followed by 'striking' accidents – that is, bumping into things, objects falling on feet … things like that.

Int'er: So presumably there are some basic guidelines for making the home a safer place for children?

C.M.: Yes, there are some simple rules which are easy to follow. First of all, chemicals and medicines are safe if used properly but can cause harm if swallowed, so they need to be stored properly and out of reach. Secondly, electricity can be dangerous if used incorrectly.

Int'er: Yes, please tell us more about that, Corina.

C.M.: Well, overloading powerpoints with too many appliances is risky, and not checking the condition of your electrical equipment is extremely dangerous.

Int'er: Everything you say is very obvious, isn't it?

C.M.: Oh, yes, but people don't think an accident could happen to them.

Int'er: What other things should we be aware of?

C.M.: Well, a great many children have accidents involving fires. They should never play with matches or lighters, and if there's a bonfire in the garden, children should be supervised at all times.

Int'er: And, of course, it's important that they understand that fire is not a toy.

C.M.: Definitely. But not just fires – don't forget hot ovens and hot drinks! Hot drinks can scald up to half an hour after being made.

Int'er: Corina, thank you very much for pointing out some of the hazards which we, and particularly children, may face in the home. I, for one, will think twice next time I cook a meal.

Unit 9: Listening, Exercise 10

Track 3

Listen to this interview with an Indian classical dancer and follow the instructions in your Workbook. You will hear the interview twice.

Interviewer: Good evening to our listeners and to our special guest this evening – Dr Sinduri Jayasinghe, the famous Indian classical dancer.

Dr Jayasinghe: Good evening, and thank you for inviting me.

Int'er: Now, Dr Jayasinghe, our listeners are waiting to hear about your career as a professional Indian classical dancer. What can you tell us?

Dr J.: Well, it all started at the theatre, where I was born.

Int'er: You were born in a theatre?

Dr J.: Yes! My mother was actually at the theatre watching a performance when she gave birth to me.

Int'er: How did you become interested in dancing?

Dr J.: I started learning classical dance forms that originated in southern India at a very early age. I became famous when I danced the 'Arangetram', which is a very crucial performance for a dancer.

Int'er: Why is this dance, the Arangetram, so important?

Dr J.: It is a special offering by the debutante to her teacher, family, friends and critics. The performance can have a great impact on the dancer's career, as the judgement of the critics is crucial. Fortunately, the response was extremely complimentary about me, and I was even raved about by the critics and media alike.

Int'er: What happened after that?

Dr J.: Well, since then, I have had the unique distinction of making over 1,600 live performances, besides being one of the youngest dancers invited to dance at the prestigious residence of the President of India. Also, I am a graduate from the Madras Music College and I was selected best dancer of Tamil Nadu state in 1984.

Int'er: Tell us something about your training.

Dr J.: Since the age of three, I have had intensive training from Mr Pillai, who is one of the leading dance gurus of India. His style of teaching includes history, theory, dance music, development and dance technique.

Int'er: What else do you do in your busy schedule?

Dr J.: Well, I choreograph all of my own productions, as well as dance programmes for other artists in different dance forms, such as Indian folk dances and many other traditional folk dances of India and Sri Lanka.

Int'er: Do you teach a particular age or ability?

Dr J.: No. I love to teach dance to all those interested, irrespective of their age and ability. I particularly enjoy teaching children and the poor. I have been teaching girls from impoverished homes for free, as my contribution to society.

Int'er: That is wonderful. Could you tell us something about your dance performances?

Dr J.: Well, I have been an 'A' grade artist for over ten years in Indian television. My performances have been televised a number of times on the *National Programme of Music and Dance* and on regional programmes. As a young dancer, I proved that I was capable of dancing solo for three hours at a stretch to an audience of dance connoisseurs. Also, I am the lead dancer of my own group of 60 performers. Since 1986, I have toured the United Kingdom, France, Germany, the former Soviet Union, Canada, Singapore, Malaysia, Japan and the USA. Finally, I am an artist for the Indian Council of Cultural Relations of the Indian government, which sends members throughout the world as goodwill ambassadors to promote Indian culture.

Int'er: Well, Dr Jayasinghe, that is certainly an amazing career. I would like to thank you on behalf of myself and our listeners for being with us today.

Unit 10: Listening

Listen to this interview about a mathematical discovery and then answer the questions in your Workbook. You will hear the interview twice.

Interviewer:	On this week's *Science in Action* programme, we welcome Professor Emilia Pavlida, a mathematics specialist. Good morning, Professor.
Professor Pavlida:	Good morning, Thomas.
Int'er:	Professor, can you tell us exactly what a prime number is?
Prof. P.:	A prime number is any number which can only be divided by itself and 1; for example, 5, 23 and 101.
Int'er:	So ... 9 would not be a prime number because it can be divided by 3, as well as by itself and 1?
Prof. P.:	That's right.
Int'er:	So why are they so important? What is all the fuss about?
Prof. P.:	Primes are important to mathematicians because they help in the study of codes, which has become an increasingly relevant topic with the rise in importance of the Internet.
Int'er:	So should I be using my spare time to find prime numbers?
Prof. P.:	No, it would probably be a complete waste of time. The most recently discovered prime number was over four million digits in length and ...
Int'er:	I'm sorry, did you say over four million digits in length?
Prof. P.:	Yes! There are computers searching 24 hours a day to find the next biggest prime. In the time it would take you to write out four million digits – say, three weeks – another prime might have been found!
Int'er:	Amazing!
Prof. P.:	And there are cash prizes to be won by the person whose computer finds it!
Int'er:	Cash prizes? How much money is being offered?
Prof. P.:	There is a competition at the moment which is offering 100,000 dollars to the first person to find a ten-million-digit prime number. A few years ago, 50,000 dollars was awarded for the first million-digit prime number discovered.
Int'er:	So who found the most recent biggest prime number?
Prof. P.:	Well, there are more than 130,000 volunteers and their computers using special programs that examine different numbers to see whether they are prime. The latest 'largest prime' was discovered by a computer belonging to Michael Cameron, a 20-year-old Canadian. It took 45 days to find!
Int'er:	So why was Mr Cameron searching for the prime?

Appendix

Prof. P.: A friend had informed him that if he was going to leave his computer on all the time, he should make use of it, so he put the software program on his computer. Forty-five days later, his computer found the prime number.

Int'er: Professor, how many prime numbers are there, or don't we know?

Prof. P.: New primes are being discovered at the rate of about one a year, and we have no idea how many there are.

Int'er: And all I need is an Internet connection and the special computer program?

Prof. P.: Yes, and a lot of patience!

Int'er: Professor Pavlida, thank you very much for your time.

Prof. P.: You're welcome, and good luck in your search for the first ten-million-digit prime number!

Track 5

Unit 14: Listening, Exercise 11

Listen to this interview about the world's smallest lizard and answer the questions in your Workbook. You will hear the interview twice.

Interviewer: Good evening, and welcome to *The Animal Show*. Today, we welcome Stefano Maloni, a conservationist who has recently returned from the Caribbean. Stefano, tell us about the amazing work that you're doing.

Stefano Maloni: Well, we've just discovered a lizard which lives on Isla Beata – a small, forest-covered island in the Caribbean. At just 16 millimetres from nose to tail, the Jaragua is the world's smallest lizard. It was discovered by us at three different sites, and we believe that the lizard lives only in these areas.

Int'er: Why is finding this particular lizard so important?

S.M.: Because it's quite likely that the Jaragua is about as small as a land animal can be. There are about 23,000 species of reptile, bird and mammal across the world. Smaller animals have a danger of dying out because of the small size of their bodies, as well as the minimum size needed for a functioning nervous system.

Int'er: Do you think the Jaragua is the smallest lizard out there?

S.M.: No, I don't. I think that there are other tiny lizards, but the Jaragua will hold the record for some time. It's not likely that we'll encounter a smaller one in the near future.

Int'er: Are there any other small animals in the Caribbean?

S.M.: Yes, there are. The Caribbean is also home to the world's smallest bird, frog and snake. We think that these small animals could become popular environmental selling points, as they would appeal to children. It is very important to make people aware that only ten per cent of the Caribbean's original forests remain, and a wave of extinction may soon hit the region. We're going to have losses, and it is only a matter of time.

Int'er: How do you feel about the future of the Caribbean?

S.M.:   I feel optimistic about the Jaragua lizard because Isla Beata is part of a national park and local people have formed conservation organisations. The park's remoteness and ruggedness give it further protection. Of course, there are dangers for the lizard because of its size. Because it is so small, it lives like an insect and feeds on other small insects. It must be on guard against being eaten by predators, such as centipedes and scorpions.

Int'er: Stefano, thank you very much for joining us today. Good luck in the future with your environmental campaigns.

Track 6

Unit 15: Listening

Listen to this talk about the future of DVDs and then answer the questions in your Workbook. You will hear the talk twice.

To begin with, we had records: you know, those big black discs which got scratched so easily – but at least if one side was ruined, you could always play the other side! Then, in the late 1960s, audio cassettes became the thing to be seen with, and our roadsides became host to kilometre after kilometre of unwanted brown tape. There were video cassettes as well, and they seem to have survived better than their audio counterparts. Next, about 20 years on, in the early 1990s, compact discs, or CDs to you and me, arrived. At greater expense, of course, and they have been around ever since. But soon they too are going to disappear without a trace, just as records and cassettes have done.

A more recent arrival, still somewhat misunderstood by older people, is the DVD. It looks exactly like the CDs you insert in your computer at home or work. DVDs are quickly destroying video, which could soon become completely obsolete. Now, experts in the music industry are predicting that, within the next ten years, DVD A ('A' stands for 'audio') will have done the same to CDs.

So, what are the advantages of using DVDs? Well, firstly, instead of playing in only two tracks (stereo), a DVD can play in six, giving you as close to 'pure sound' as is currently possible. This advance in sound quality is far greater than when we moved from cassette to CD. The difference is amazing. Secondly, the amount of storage space is very important. A single DVD is capable of holding more than eight times the information that a normal CD can; if you 'layer' them (put two DVDs one on top of the other in one disc), this increases the capacity even more. If you remove moving pictures from a DVD (about 95 per cent of the storage on a DVD video is pictures), the space for sound is vast. A DVD audio book could hold the entire *Harry Potter* series.

But, as always, there are drawbacks as well. A DVD will not play in any equipment other than that specified as a DVD player – in other words, unfortunately, you can't play a DVD in a CD player. So that means a lot of extra expense because you'll need a new DVD player for films, another one for your sound system, another one in the car, a personal player for when you go jogging, and so on. Also, currently, the facility to record on a DVD is still quite primitive and, while DVD recorders are available, they are still relatively expensive.

Appendix

Unit 19: Listening, Exercise 9

Listen to this interview with a Marketing Assistant in the fashion world and answer the questions in your Workbook. You will hear the interview twice.

Interviewer:	Today, on *Fashion Plus*, we're very pleased to welcome Natasha Kafouros, winner of this year's Fashion Marketing award. Natasha, tell us something about how you got your current job.
Natasha Kafouros:	Hello, Manuel. Well, I had always wanted to get into fashion and I applied for my first job when I saw a website advert. I was interviewed and got the job as PA to the Marketing Director in a large fashion company. Shortly after I started, a vacancy came up for the Marketing Assistant role in the same company, so I decided to try for it and got it!
Int'er:	Why do you think you were so suitable for the job?
N.K.:	I had a lot of relevant work experience before I got this job, which helped me gain experience in the industry. Also, I was able to build up a large contacts list, which is really useful in the fashion business. I think that really helped me.
Int'er:	How important was it that you went to university?
N.K.:	It's very important to have a degree because it gives you lots of different skills that are vital in the working world.
Int'er:	Such as?
N.K.:	Well, communication skills, computer skills and, most importantly for my job, meeting deadlines!
Int'er:	What steps would you recommend to someone who wanted to go into the world of fashion?
N.K.:	Firstly, get as much work experience as you can, in lots of different areas of the industry, so you can see which part you want to go into. Definitely create a contacts book and put absolutely everyone you meet in it – you never know when you might need them!
Int'er:	That sounds like excellent advice. What else?
N.K.:	Always be on the lookout for jobs and opportunities. Spread the word that you are looking for something, and make yourself invaluable during work experience so that people will remember you! The fashion industry is not as fickle as you may think ...
Int'er:	What do you mean, exactly?
N.K.:	They know what they want and what they are looking for, so don't be scared to push your way in if you think you have what they want. The industry doesn't change easily. Don't be shy. It's much better to be confident, because this is another excellent way of making people remember you.

Int'er: Natasha, what other advice can you give our listeners?

N.K.: Be open to all the different areas of fashion; for example, public relations, styling, writing, marketing, buying, and so on. Try not to limit your options, especially at the beginning. And finally, read lots of fashion magazines, because this will help you to stay 'on the pulse' and remain in touch with all aspects of the business.

Acknowledgements

The author and publishers are grateful for the text permissions granted to reproduce texts in either the original or adapted form. While every effort has been made, it has not always been possible to identify the sources of all the materials used, or to trace all copyright holders. If any omissions are brought to our notice, we will be happy to include the appropriate acknowledgements on reprinting.

pp. 9–10 adapted from an article by Tim Radford, copyright Guardian News & Media Ltd, 2001; p. 11 adapted from an article by Helena Smith in *The Guardian Weekly*, 2001; p. 17 adapted from www.vrg.org, 2004; p. 19 © The Economist Newspaper Limited, London, 2004; p. 24 adapted from www.fau.org.uk, 2004; p. 34 adapted from www.home-ed.vic.edu.au, 2002; pp. 40–41 © Suzannah Oliver/NI Syndication Limited, 2001; p. 42 adapted from en.wikipedia.org, 2008; pp. 46–47 adapted from 'Monkeys lend a "Helping Hand"' by Elizabeth Lund, first published in *The Christian Science Monitor*, 2005; p. 49 adapted from 'Taking the Fear out of Presentations' by Ahmed Al-Ajmi, from *Youth Observer*, Oman, 2007; p. 54 adapted from www.moscowtimes.ru, 2004; p. 63 adapted from www.sciencenews.org and www.mcmua.com, 2003; p. 67 adapted from an article by Tania Branigan, © Guardian News & Media Ltd, 2001; p. 68 © NI Syndication, 2006; p. 72 adapted from an article by Steve Connor, copyright *The Independent*, 2001; p. 74 adapted from 'An Inconvenient Height Above Sea Level' by Marc Owen Jones in *Bahrain & Beyond*, published by Magnum-Bigg, 2007; p. 78 adapted from 'Hues of Henna' by Sarah White-Bait Al Zuhair in *Wings of Oman*, 2006; pp. 80–81 adapted from www.npaid.org, 2008; p. 84 adapted from www.wpro.who.int, 2007; p. 104 adapted from 'Kathakali and Coconuts' by Mark Daffey in *Open Skies*, 2006; p. 111 adapted from an article by Anna Johnson for Associated Press Archive, 2007, used with permission of the Associated Press © 2008, all rights reserved; p. 118 adapted from www.communityonline.com, 2008.

All photographs are provided by Alamy: p. 29(*t*) mediablitzimages (UK) Limited; p. 29(*b*) amana images inc.; p. 60(*t*) Marco Secchi; p. 60(*b*) Sue Wilson; p. 79(*l*) Peter Alvey; p. 79(*c*) curved-light; p. 79(*tr*) MaRoDee Photography; p.79(*br*) D. Hurst; p. 91 David Sanger Photography; p. 122 Iconotec.

Key: t = *top,* b = *bottom,* c = *centre,* l = *left,* r = *right. These letters are also used in combination.*